Artisan of the Human Spirit

Awakening to Life's Lessons

Artisan of the Human Spirit

Awakening to Life's Lessons

Tony Anders

© Copyright Tony Anders 2010

All rights reserved. No part of this book may be reproduced in any manner whatsoever without written permission. Printed in the United States of America.

Paperback ISBN 978-0-578-05351-6

Hardback ISBN 978-0-557-39583-5

Contents

Acknowledgements xi

Preface xiii

Introduction xvii

The Fort 1
Reflections 7

The Black Book 9
Reflections 16

Poolside 17
Reflections 21

The Calling 23
Reflections 28

Race Car Driver 29
Reflections 33

It's Not Just For Sundays Anymore 35
Reflections 40

The Storm 41
Reflections 47

The World Is Flat And The Sky Is Falling 49
Reflections 54

Look Inside	**55**
Reflections	60
If It Weren't For You, I'd Be Happy	**61**
Reflections	65
Remember To Love The One You're With	**67**
Reflections	71
The Beacon	**73**
Reflections	78
She Burnt The Eggs	**79**
Reflections	84
I Choose To Not Participate	**85**
Reflections	89
The Rest Is Just Gravy	**91**
Reflections	97
Why Not?	**99**
Reflections	104
Quite The Experience	**105**
Reflections	109
It's An As-Is Deal	**111**
Reflections	115
Letting It Go	**117**
Reflections	122

Please Don't Change **123**
   Reflections 128

Alone In A Crowd **129**
   Reflections 134

Fragments **135**
   Reflections 140

Something Greater **141**
   Reflections 147

Cut! **149**
   Reflections 153

Bookends **155**
   Reflections 160

Be Prepared **161**
   Reflections 167

Final Thoughts **169**

About the Title **171**

*To Dana, Alexa, & Austin
My raisons d'être*

Acknowledgements

How do you truly acknowledge everyone who has contributed to your story? Whether it is a *bit* part, the role of an *extra*, or a *lead* role that remains for the whole story, or perhaps enters then exits strategically, I find it impossible to significantly acknowledge or thank anyone.

From teachers early on in my life, to the people who challenged my faith, to those I hope remain absent from my life, I am still grateful for the parts they played in my development and in how I got to where I am today. Their absence would make my story a different one. The not-so-pleasant people, places and things would contribute to possibly me being weaker in some form in my ability to either accept life's issues or overcome my adversaries, and those who arrived with blessings; my life may be that much less abundant and fulfilling.

The words in this book total over fifty-thousand; I could replace them all with the names of people who have come and gone, who remained, who have taken and given to me, who have inspired me, or caused me great distress. It is those persons I thank, each and every one, for their contribution to my collective whole, my story, and my current state. You all have a special place regardless of the role you played.

I confess I am here and a better man because of my parents. I am stronger, grateful, and perhaps still alive because of the unwavering love of my wonderful wife, Dana. My beautiful, beautiful children, Alexa and Austin, remind me that I hold one of the greatest titles available to a man: Daddy. To everyone else, you hold no less a position. I thank you for your presence, your gifts, your wisdom, and even your storms.

If I had it all to do over again, from where I now stand, I would not change a thing.

Preface

What I am not: I am not a doctor. I am not a professor. I am not an author with an expansive list of inspirational or self-help books adorning shelves of popular bookstores. I do not claim to hold any titles or authority over anyone. I am not a specialist and I am not a professional counselor.

I say this up front to give leverage to the reasons I wrote this book. I make no claim to be anything other than a human being who genuinely cares about his fellow man. Which now leads to what I am: I am a regular guy from Washington Court House, a small town in south-central Ohio. When I resided there, it boasted a population of around 13,000. It is a small, friendly community with an economy supported by local agriculture, a handful of industrial firms; small locally owned businesses, and some national chains. I lived there until my high-school graduation, after which I moved to the state capital of Columbus; and since then, I have resided in a few of the city suburbs.

I am the father of two beautiful children; both are blessings in my life. I have a wife of fourteen years; we have been together for nineteen. She is a wonderful person who deserves one of the good seats in heaven for dealing with me all these years.

I own a home, a business, autos, and have a dog. I have grown roots, as well have traveled. I have toys as well as debt, and am of average looks and build. I have as many blessings as challenges, many friends (perhaps a few who may not feel the same), and can claim successes and failures, good health and illness, pain and loss. All these things I list here to simply, generally, and humbly, support my claim that I am a "regular guy." No better than you, no worse than you, and yet one of you.

On the positive side, I have been blessed with positions of leadership, education, and the ability to get my thoughts and messages to the public through print and other media. I've always considered my core gift to be that of *communication* and the ability to identify with people in all dispositions and walks of life.

I feel I may hold one simple qualification. Up to this point, my career has been in the beauty industry, where I have spent twenty-plus years listening to people's stories. Stories of beauty, love, hate, victory, failure, failed marriages, menstrual cramps, murder, etc. Like a bartender, I lend a neutral ear. I may interject a thought or some simple wisdom. After an hour so, we will say good-bye. At that point if not emotionally feeling better or more connected, at least feeling prettier, tidier, or stylish.

The personal stories and interactions with my clients ignited my passion for listening and communication. They fueled my desire to help people beyond what grows from forehead to nape. Often times I was the only available or compassionate party some people had to turn to. I found, and find, I genuinely and truly give a damn.

In my career as a hairstylist, I eventually became an instructor, writer, motivator, new-talent coach, media personality, and consumer advocate. These elements put me in touch with many people and organizations, and strengthened my desire to use what resources I had, to do what I could, to help people and make a difference.

It seemed that in spiritual matters, it took money and almost celebrity status to obtain a certain level of wisdom or attunement. I believed when I reached *that* level, I would then have arrived at peace, would become self-sufficient and spiritually connected, and then be able to pass it onward.

I sought motivators, teachers, classes, books, systems, mentors, and gurus, on a never-ending quest to obtain the perfect *system.* I wanted to teach others the key to overcoming obstacles, the key to feeling better about themselves, and the key to finding happiness. I listened to so many "prophets"—speakers, authors, and talk show hosts—who have hordes of followers and believers. They wrote books and people bought the books. They made DVDs and people bought the DVDs. My insatiable thirst of needing what others had would perpetually lead me to yet another source—something I didn't yet have but wanted to obtain. After all, how could I help others or myself without these secrets? How was I to grow, be important, a better leader, and be sought as a guru without these elusive keys?

I felt that after all the books I read, the classes I attended, the people I spoke with, and the years I spent in my career, I felt like I was pouring water in a bucket with a hole in it. I studied the writings of some of the world's most brilliant minds. I absorbed their material and mantras—yet that arrival—that state, always seemed to be just beyond my grasp. I often wondered how much more I had to read. How many more programs or seminars must I attend? How many more life stories must I listen to? How many more personal successes or failures must

I endure? Where was God or *my* spiritual connection? Where was happiness? Where was the end of pain? What ended suffering? Where was abundance? Was it possible? I know now, it is.

In retrospect, I realize I was fishing in the wrong pond. I held *others* responsible for my happiness, success, and journey. I expected the others to know exactly what I needed; when I needed it; where to deliver it; and in what shape, form, quantity, and color. If something did not come to me exactly how I wanted it to, I felt I had failed or others had failed me.

I now know that the gifts I sought, I had all along. I did not need to spend the time and money I did seeking the *true* secrets of serenity, peace, awareness, and joy. It became like an Easter egg hunt. I became aware the gifts were there, and near me, so I was able to find them one by one and add them to my proverbial basket. These gifts did not always present themselves easily. At first, some were confusing and required contemplation, dissection, and digestion, for me to get the *essence* of the lessons, but I did eventually.

One of the greatest epidemics I encountered in my journey is the prevailing belief that people think they are alone in their circumstances; that no one understands. I have heard people say: "No one will talk to me." "What I have done is too awful to forgive." "There is no God (Source or Creator or however you identify with the concept at hand)."

As a *regular guy*, I can identify with a fair amount of people. I encounter the same trials and triumphs many people do. Now, I just get a return on my investment. Life pays me dividends I can reinvest and share to enrich my life and use to create physical and emotional abundance. Where others might experience pain, I now get a payoff.

Due to my history and qualifications, or lack thereof, I have chosen my avenue as one of sharing rather than coaching, teaching, advising, or counseling. It is a *therapeutic* sharing.

I find this non-threatening, non-confrontational approach works best because it does not challenge anyone's path, beliefs, religion, or practices. The stories of my personal journey will entertain and educate you. I suspect you will connect with many of them.

Instead of trying to tell others what to do, I choose to share what happened to me, how it helped me, and where I am now as a result of those circumstances. By using this approach, people can relax, recline, and absorb, while identifying with, and reflecting on their own situation.

I want everyone to know they have support. None will be judged here. No one is abandoned. I present stories of my growth—not as "six easy steps" or "years of accumulated formal education"—but as they were presented to me so that all may benefit as I did.

Introduction

My journaling was not intended to become a book. Its original purpose was to document my personal journey so I could remember and reference it, as well as someday share this exciting quest with my children. However, as my spiritual cultivation grew, so did my desire to share my discovery: one's life *can* change, on a very deep and enduring level.

For many years, I spent a lot of time, thought, and energy on trying to find myself. I remember my father telling me, "If you're trying to find yourself, reach back, grab your (butt) with both hands, and there you are." Simple, yes, but not quite what I was looking for! (Although, there is a ring of truth in his words.)

As my awareness escalated and I started to find more answers, I was able to evolve and find peace. In the past couple years; I have endured a multitude of challenges, crises, illnesses, and other situations that tested my resolve. I found I no longer sought titles. I no longer sought the grail of wisdom from the experts. I realized there was something more. There was something for me, and to receive certain things, I had to share certain things.

I remember one night having a discussion with a friend. The topic of who or what I truly wanted to be came up. My response came quickly and without hesitation. I stated, "I want to be an artisan of the human spirit." My friend simply raised his brows and said, "Wow, that's cool!" I knew then, my journey had begun.

My observations are about simple things that happen to most of us in a normal day. They are not meant to be profound, which is the beauty of what I present. I observe simple "moments of truth" where we encounter situations that unfold before us daily. These situations are where we have an opportunity to learn and gain knowledge about ourselves, and perhaps eliminate suffering.

Often we look for this bright light or an earth-shattering lesson to get our attention. However, I have found that the most enduring and deep messages occur in the subtlest of circumstances.

What I share are examples of my moments—not to suggest that yours will appear in the same context. Once I realized what I needed to hear or see was often already in my presence, my evolution began. The more tuned in to this I became, the more the messages appeared and coincidentally, the more I found myself in a state of gratitude.

Everything in this book was initially written in longhand. I knew writing longhand helped connect the writer more to his or her work, and I did not want to be dependent on a battery or electricity to document my thoughts. So, I went to a local bookstore and purchased a thick, brown-leather journal with lined paper and a simple attached silk bookmark. The word *Journal* was embossed on the front cover and there were about four hundred blank pages waiting. I also bought a handful of black ink pens. I chose pens so I would not do a lot of on-the-spot editing.

Indeed, there were some scribbles, but the majority of my entries came from the Spirit, to my heart, to my pen, and then onto the paper. I always said, "I don't write, 'it' writes." This means, when called or inspired, I would sit, momentarily reflect, and then write each entry uninterrupted. They were usually eight to twelve handwritten pages. I would not read or edit them upon completion. I would make a little glyph or scribble on the page to signify when I was done, return my utensils and glasses to my book bag, and proceed with my day. Aside from simple courtesy edits, grammar, and punctuation, the original writings remain true as I wrote them, not for their award-winning prose and literary appreciation, but rather for the messages contained within. (Note: since writing this Introduction, I have had the text professionally edited.)

I knew journaling would aid me in my quest for self-awareness. I wanted to diminish my ego's influence in what I thought, said, and did. I wanted to be aware of its infiltration in my life and writing my thoughts down would be a good way for me to take inventory. I wanted to know when emotions such as anger, jealousy, and resentment tried to get a hold of me and practice my awareness of those instances. For example I observed: *I* am not angry, but *I* am the *awareness* that sees the anger attacking my human form. If I can detach and take a different perspective, the outcome will be more therapeutic and beneficial to me.

Writing allows me to detach and observe my actions and contemplate the positive or negative consequences. It systematically documents my reactions and emotions in a certain situation and allows me to see where ego may have negatively played a role. In my reflective analysis, I can see where a different path of action could have been observed, perceived, or taken, thus allowing growth in the future. If I did not become aware in time for one situation, I might be aware the next time. I also try to alleviate judgments and any retribution upon myself and simply observe the journey. I remain distant yet connected, with an underlying love and a desire for spiritual growth and to better myself. I become my own observer, teacher, and guardian.

After letting these essays sit for some time, I read them and realized my journey could possibly benefit others. People could insert their own personalities or locations to identify with the message. I wrote them to be vivid descriptions to place you there by my side to help you in essence walk with me. So, think of this book as a fireside chat where the stories are meant to entertain as well as inspire. My writing is a gesture of love. It is my outstretched hand. No struggle needs to be endured alone. It is not that we fall, but that we rise up again! I hope these stories entertain, inspire, and provide light upon everyone's path. Ultimately, I offer them as a "smile and nudge" in a new direction!

Although I have added an introductory statement to each essay (italicized text), the essays themselves have not been manipulated. Their original message remains intact. And, at the end of each essay, I have added questions to help aid in reflection in one's life and circumstances. There is some space to write; but I encourage everyone to start a journal so that the responses are not limited by the space available in this book.

The Essays

The Fort

In life, not every classroom has a desk, nor every church a steeple!

*I loved this essay as I was capturing a special moment that happened to me. Although I cannot choose a favorite, due to the fact a message's impact will be different depending on where a person **is** at the time of reading, this essay is special due to the simple fact it was my first time putting pen to paper for my own benefit. Not only was I trying to create a vivid written recollection, but I wanted to share the impact it had upon me.*

This essay captures, for me, a shift. As I wrote, I realized a shift in perception can create a shift in an experience. I saw where my perception of the situation and my ability to get outside of my own head, if even for a brief while, created a special and significant moment for me. The moments I described, now upon reflection, are much more magical to me. Regretfully, in my older ways of thinking, perhaps something like exploring with my son may have seemed trivial or cumbersome, or perhaps would not have occurred to this degree. However, by surrendering to living in the moment, I was able to have a special experience. A moment that I wish I were able to have had being a son myself, but now was blessed with a second chance.

I am blessed with two children. My daughter Alexa is ten years old; my son, Austin, is five. Alexa is athletic and active. She has played soccer for a handful of years and has developed it into a budding passion.

On many evenings and weekends, Austin and I are a captive audience on the sidelines of a soccer game or practice, as my wife often works during my "soccer mom" obligations. I felt badly for my son, realizing he would rather be home playing video games—or pretty much anywhere else as opposed to waiting on Sissy. To no avail, Austin often found his desires trumped, and he accompanied me to frequent games and practices.

Spring season allowed the local parks to be the site of said activities, one in particular, Thompson Park, is the setting for many soccer practices and games in our community. It is a well-manicured, beautiful expanse of fields and play structures, with hills to aid in spectator comfort and tree lines that separated the playfields.

The trees are lush, full, and inviting to adventurous minds. They are the type a kid could easily hide, climb, and escape in, with all the wonder fueling an active imagination. The brush at the bottom of the trees is thick and full and creates a perfect division between the fields. Random manmade openings, and some created by the active imaginations of young explorers, allow foot traffic to pass through. Other trails were created over time by people awkwardly finding their way through the trees and underbrush. In the most yielding of pathways, through a mixture of young and mature trees, you can find bushes, stones, and patches of barren ground. It is littered with nature's compost of leaves and twigs and is punctuated by random branches that have fallen.

One warm, sunny evening my daughter was practicing on a field flanked by a tree line that sprawled right to left approximately one hundred yards, and was about as wide as half a football field with a tree height around sixty feet. A sidewalk went through the middle and, on the other side of the sidewalk; nature continued and repeated this majestic divider for another hundred yards.

My son and I were milling about with about an hour to kill, so we went in search of some stimulation. During games we would show our sideline support, at least I would; Austin would play games on my iPhone. We cheered with the other parents if it happened to be a game. During practices, however, we often did our own thing to entertain ourselves, trying to appeal to the quick-to-bore mind of a five-year-old.

As we walked along the aforementioned sidewalk, I noticed to my left an opening in the tree line that was approximately six feet high and three feet wide—definitely inviting us to enter. It was apparent others had ventured before, although the opening was not obvious unless you happened to look in that direction. Even though we were not dressed for the woods, both in cargo shorts, no socks, and me in a polo shirt and my son in a T-shirt, nature beckoned and we answered.

The growth was full, lush, and green allowing only sporadic rays of sunlight through. The branches allowed just enough sun to dance about the floor of the wooded area choreographed by the gentle evening wind. Austin quickly found a stick that became his walking companion. It was as crooked as a dog's hind leg, but I thought, "Are there really any written rules to walking sticks?" I noticed I was sinking into a long-lost appreciation for moments of my childhood—the innocence of a "who-cares, let's-explore" attitude. All that mattered was happening then and there. My son was "Lewis" and I was "Clark."

The symphony of birds chirping and the whisper of the wind rustling the leaves dominated our journey's soundtrack. Even though we were close to the cheers and guttural yells from the coaches, the acoustics in our new world made all the noises appear miles away. I can hear the crunch of the brush, the snap of small twigs, and the soft carefree humming of my son. How I could hear these soft sounds over the screams of kids yelling and whistles was magical, and yet had a special acoustic sensation I appreciated.

We came to a small clearing about halfway in surrounded by numerous trees with trunks the diameter of a car's hubcap. Dense brush and bushes flanked the path and opening. Many branches had fallen, sheared from the tops of the elder trees during recent storms and had created piles that reminded me of toppled bowling pins. My son was milling about picking up stones, branches, and other trinkets that dirtied his inquisitive fingers only to be cleansed with an innocent brush of the hand against his pant leg. He looked up at me with a grin and said, "We're buddies, aren't we Dad?" I replied, "You know it, pal!" I knew our simple walk was becoming a bonding experience, one that I do not recall having in my young life with my dad, but something I had always longed for. The meaningless stuff seems to mean the most.

A few sturdy branches, about three to five feet in length, rather straight and the diameter about the size of an orange, were strewn about. I decided to create a teepee. Actually it was three sticks in a pyramid, but to a five-year-old it was a testimony of my years of wisdom and a gift from the gods of architecture, validated with a "Coooooool!" Austin proceeded to adorn the foot of each branch of our pyramid with rocks he carefully selected, placing them with the precision of a young engineer. I continued gathering branches, filling in our creation to give it more substance and strength, more sticks, more stones. I was a kid again, gathering like a pilgrim building his log cabin, or a survivor on a desert island.

I had a strange determination to create something for my son, as if it was in our backyard, as if it was our woods, our creation, and our moment. My energy was abundant, and the job seemed effortless. Austin kept interjecting our task with an occasional, "We are buddies, aren't we Dad?" And I replied with my standard response, "You know it, pal!" Which was acknowledged with a quiet "hmm" of appreciation, a smile, and then it was back to work. After forty-five minutes or so we had built a lattice of branches, caverns, walls, and teepees that would make a tribal elder proud. We gathered, placed, evaluated, replaced, and built our "Fortress of Solitude" for a private membership of two—the "buddies."

I don't know what it is about young boys, but they retain liquid. My son is king at having to "go" at inopportune times. Nature called, he answered, christening the ground behind the original teepee, which from then on was designated "the bathroom." A few more additions and adjustments brought us to an awareness that Sissy was about done with soccer. Our journey was fading back to a reality I didn't want to enter. I sat for a moment in silent reflection of our adventure and was joined by my son. His arms struggled to reach the height of my shoulder as he exclaimed, "I love you, Dad!" "I love you too, pal," I responded.

The joy was overcome with the melancholy realization that we had to leave our fort behind. This masterpiece, this testimony to a father and son, it was ours yet we had to leave it behind. It was back to the car, back home, to homework, to baths, to our normal routine. The story was over.

I grabbed my phone and took a couple pictures of my son with his arms spread with pride and artistic triumph. We ventured onward to retrieve Sissy, back to the real world, wondering how long our fortress would remain before succumbing to vandals, nature, or both. It was heartbreaking leaving our creation behind as my son wanted to show the world, as did I, our creation. I thought it was the fort that mattered. I was wrong.

A couple days went by and soccer practice once again came into the rotation of our lives' schedule. Alexa asked me if I had been back to see our fort. In asking, she had a look, a concerned look, to tell me what I already knew upon her posing that simple question. It had only taken three days for vandals to destroy our fort.

I thought it would bother me, but all along I had a feeling the fort wouldn't last long. I guess the hopeless romantic in me pictured another father and son coming by to only improve upon our design; creating an eventual Robinson Crusoe structure for all to enjoy. I am a realist, a hopeless romantic, and not a pessimist, and although a bit saddened temporarily, I see it as a clean slate calling for another adventure; another reason to return to my childhood once again.

The lesson I learned was interesting: I have no control over what can happen. I need to savor each moment, and drink in as much of the present to leave an indelible stamp on my memory to where nothing has to fade or be lost. The better my presence is now, the better my recall is later. In the past, I tried to hold on to things for their sentimental value, but I realize the values I place upon the objects themselves are insignificant to the value they retain in my memory and the memory of others.

The images from that day are vividly stored in my mind, heart, and spirit. I have them forever, and in sacred condition, untouchable for eternity. In that memory, it is not the fort I cherish; it is the precious time I shared with my son. In that memory, Austin will always be five years old, I will be the brave explorer; we will be buddies, and the fort: enduring.

We are destined to have things come and go in our lives, and we often place too much identification of who we are in those things, and we sometimes feel if we lose those things, we lose the memories attached to them as well. Things are fleeting and their value diminishes, but the human experiences and our ability to remain vividly connected to those experiences through our memories does not have to leave us.

True, it is difficult to lose items in times of disaster, theft, or loss, but we do not have to lose the value of the experience they represent. Mementos and objects connect to the ego and not to the spiritual blessing that placed them in our lives in the first place. I have had and lost many things, money, and titles. To some that fort may have been a simple pile of dead or dying organic material, scattered, without value, and forgotten—but to two "little boys" lost in a moment, it was priceless, even if only for short time. I realize there is no greater thing I acquired that day, or any day since, than the title of "buddy."

A few months after writing this, I revisited it for the first time. I was able to go back to that moment. It was emotional for me, as I experienced a state of gratitude for the ability not only to have had the experience and to be able to share it with my son, but also for the ability to feel and see the blessings therein. This experience showed me the importance of being present and to realize what is of true value in this world. When the simplest of moments are shared, they can become genuinely special.

I implore you to be where you are when you are there, and to also realize that what may be tedious or boring to one, can be monumentally significant to another. Some things may seem unimportant now, but once put into spatial perspective with the passing of time, these experiences can become treasures.

Reflections

Are there times when my pre-conceived perspective on a situation has created a less than desirable outcome for me?

What can I do to change that in the future?

Are there times when a positive outlook on my participation in something I was uninterested in may have created a better experience for others and possibly me?

Can I get beyond my feelings and enjoy what may seem inconvenient, tedious or a bother now, and allow it to become a treasured memory?

Am I willing to seek another truth, perspective, or viewpoint on things that now may be difficult for me?

Am I willing to explore different ways of approaching situations, even if the benefits may not appear until much later or only benefit people other than myself?

In what ways do I feel my life and relationships would improve if I looked at certain situations differently?

The Black Book

At times we have to lose something we cherish to appreciate its true value, or perhaps see its worthlessness.

*This was a very intense and deep moment for me as this essay developed. I was in a positive state, things were very much going my way, but a deep, insightful moment got a hold of me and profoundly enriched who I am now. This essay is a look at ego and priorities, and how in a moment's notice, they can shift dramatically. It showed me a side to appreciation and how **context** can place spiritual value on items and circumstances. I remembered how this episode called for me to quickly write and share this moment. As I read it for editing, it still took my breath away and brought back the shift I felt take place within me. I also realized "lessons" appear any time, any place, and do not necessarily come in remedy of a bad situation. The messages we are meant to receive do not always come packaged as we would expect or want them to. Salvation and spirituality are not always found in a church or sacred place, however after the intended "lesson" is received, does it not then make the item, place, or person that much more sacred?*

I am lucky in the fact that my life's schedule, although full, does not restrict me entirely from getting some me time. I do yoga and attend self-improvement meetings. I go to movies, read, and relax, as well as attend to the needs of my company and its related obligations. The remaining majority of my time is spent with my wife and kids. I really like being home and spending quality time with my wife and children. They give me a sense of purpose and gratitude. I also appreciate those rare occasions when I get a guy day: a day when nothing but selfish, self-serving tasks dominates my agenda. I often find myself bored or puzzled on how to fill the day's itinerary as these days are few and far between.

I was recently blessed with one of these gifts of solitude when my daughter's soccer team was scheduled to play in a Memorial Day weekend tournament. It was scheduled in Indianapolis, which is more than three hours from our home. My wife offered to accompany the team as I was obligated to work that weekend—until a small happenstance of serendipity opened up my schedule at the last minute. I was supposed to watch and tend to our five-year-old son who was spared his normal sideline requirements. I honestly was looking forward to a bit of male bonding, scratching things, video games, movies, cooking out, and random guy stuff Mom would not approve of.

My sister and brother-in-law offered to watch Austin overnight. This would allow me a quiet night, as well as to awaken fresh in the morning. This was still at the point when my obligation for work was still valid. Since our kids have always stayed at relatives' and friends' houses well, I did not feel neglectful.

I dropped off my son the night before, and then I enjoyed a movie, a sub, some solitude, and a restful night's sleep—expecting to retrieve my little man in the morning at his T-ball game. A yawn, stretch, and a few moments watching a home and garden show started my morning. It then developed into me trying to decide how to fill my few hours of morning freedom and sunshine prior to picking up my son.

For me, one of life's simple pleasures is the automatic outlet timer. You know, the ones you use when you go on vacation to turn your lights on and off as a security deterrent. Well, I use one to strategically start my coffee in the morning to coincide with dragging my recently awakened body into the kitchen. I remembered late the night before that I was out of coffee, and chose not to go to the store following my realization. I also rationalized that since I had the morning free and was "flying solo" as I called it, I would enjoy a trip to the local barista. After watching a TV segment on the joy of decorative pavers, I went upstairs, dressed in my dad's-day-off attire, and donned a baseball cap to hide my "pillow perm." I then loaded my pockets with the required tools: keys, cash, wallet, and watch; and hopped in the car.

I have started the practice of taking a deep inhale through my nose every time I enter into a different environment: indoors to outdoors, upstairs to downstairs, and leaving and entering buildings. It allows me to enter a presence as I smell the aromas, connect with where I am, and basically reset.

This morning, my cleansing breath was extra special as prior to my exit, my brother-in-law phoned to request an extended stay for my son, Austin, to stay with them another day and night. They were having a niece stay over and as parents know when entertaining children, two kids are often self-entertaining, and often makes it easier on the caregiver. I made sure they were cool with it, and delightfully agreed to allow him the furlough.

Hence, my morning breath was one of a free man filled with gratitude, blessing, and wonder, as I considered the possibilities of a sunny, warm, holiday weekend with no kids, wife, or direct obligation other than maybe washing a couple dishes and mowing a couple inches of grass.

Writing had developed into a pleasant pastime, and I thought of adding this task to one of my hour slots now open in my day. Plus my enjoyment of sitting and writing would be increased by surrounding myself with trimmed bushes and freshly cut grass. I love writing on my patio with soft music and birds serenading in accompaniment. This thought was in the forefront as I ventured into the street, off to obtain a few bars for my mental battery life—better known as coffee.

Along the drive, thoughts of the writing I was working on turned to the possibility of including sketches or illustrations to support the topics, something to leverage the impact and to assist the reader. I liked the idea of working with a student at the local art college. "If my work ever makes it to bookshelves, I could donate a portion to the college," I thought. I love giving and always dreamed of philanthropic endeavors.

My thought process was interrupted when I ventured into a line approximately five cars deep at the coffee shop. Fortunately, I made it a practice to have a writing instrument and paper available to me in the car and on my person in case of a spontaneous eruption of genius, or a simple mental note. I rummaged in the center console of my Honda SUV and remembered that I had recently added two small booklets of paper for memos. Both were black leather, one had a flip top and the other opened like a book. I had scribbled a few notes in the past on either important events, or me trying to appear important enough to need a memo book, but they were available and I was thankful. I chose the one that opened like a book. It was small, palm-sized, and had a ribbon to use for a bookmark. The ribbon marked where I had left off with my last notes.

As the car idled in the lane and I awaited caffeine satisfaction, I scribbled: "Definition of title" and "illustrations with local college."

I also thought and wrote: "opening quotes". I then closed the book and went through another progression and pause in the coffee line. I returned the booklet to the console, with my other arm dangling out the open window waiting my turn. I ordered two large coffees, an extra just in case, and though I would simply add my own cream at home.

I wasn't bored, but I was unoccupied, so my attention turned back to the booklet. I picked it back up and noticed approximately a dozen or so pages were previously scribbled on, so I looked to see what notes, insights or brilliance I happened to be working on in days past. At the present time I was in a state of calm, presence, and gratitude, and thought it may be fun to see what was either so urgent or important enough to inscribe upon the pages once upon a time. The first page contained my name, e-mail address, and phone number—in case I lost or misplaced it. Certainly this was going to be worth finding should it be lost or misplaced, or so I thought upon first purchase. The next few pages were penned in quick form, outside the lines, and rather sloppy. They referenced dreams I had, stuff that stroked my ego, and stuff I considered necessary: reminders of photo shoots, notes of rubbing elbows with the local who's who, putting networks together, and working on "getting out there." The facing page had random errands, trivial at best; most were marked off with a line, or scribbled through to show completion. As I looked down, staring, I noticed that none of the things I thought to be big deals at the time were graced with a line of completion. I was a brilliant dreamer, a sublime networker, and chronic procrastinator who escaped often through getting intoxicated, blaming others, and then isolating.

As I turned the page, I noticed notes on a real estate deal, others on a television appearance I must've been scripting. The small stuff was X-ed out, the big deals were untouched. On the next page were reminders for me to work on partnerships, to get in contact with friends, and to rewrite a couple dreams from the earlier pages; like my reality, though, they were slipping behind me. I thought writing them again would place emphasis on them; more pages, erratic notes, models' contact info, planning events to conquer the world, ego this, ego that. Some goals were checked, others yet to hopefully become realized, as well as a list of obligations that I was neglecting, and a major deal that possibly could have improved my future.

Ominously the next two pages were blank. I don't think I intended to keep them blank, as I would not have wasted the paper. They were not the end of my notes, but rather an interruption. They were strategically placed, and symbolically; they reflected what was happening in my life at the time. The next pages butterflied open and offered a white blankness, blue lines parallel from top to bottom, except for two words: clock radio.

I had battled addiction and substance abuse off and on for a while. My use had gone from recreational and "performance enhancing" (my definition) to destructive and spiritually crippling. I am sure that subject will lend itself to an elaboration at some other juncture, but it is not as poignant as the words clock radio and how they impacted me that morning. The previous pages of the book were reminders of obligations from the past I felt were going to make me whole and get me noticed. Clock radio; I reflected on this and repeated it several times.

I was placed in a treatment facility for "behavioral rehabilitation" after being confronted by my wife for becoming the human wreckage and the antithesis of what I spiritually sought and desired for my life. What I thought was going to be a three-day battle of the wits and will before a victorious release, turned into a fifty-six-day reprogramming adventure.

What hit me upon reading clock radio is that I remember writing it as I sat in a barren dorm, sad and broken, looking around at the institutional setting, alone, depressed, and toxic. I was afraid. I remember one of the techs telling me I was not allowed to use the phone or television and that I had to ask to go anywhere and that I could not be alone. She said if I made a list, they would approve or deny it, call my wife, and after a few days my wish might be granted. All I could muster, all I wanted, all that could come to mind was a clock radio. I wanted music, time, and connection to the outside world. I would have given a king's ransom for one. It was denied. No radios allowed. I only got the clock, and it was some time before I got my clock radio. It is funny how my desires and focus had shifted so monumentally in twenty-four hours.

The next pages of my booklet were dedicated to spirituality, beliefs, and finding joy. Questions like: "Where is my joy?" and "What do I see when I look in the mirror?" were now important to me. I drank it in like a thirsty man finding a well in the desert. The successive pages had yet another expanded wish list that included more items but still simple things—pillows and blankets from home, a shaver, and basic toiletries dominated the list. What hit me in the car that morning is that the items I listed, both the tangible and intangible, the items that connected me to my humanity and dignity, the items I needed and desired for my human spiritual connection—I had all along—but in that setting, they became some of the most important desires I could conjure.

The next pages were notes I'd written about friends I had made with phone numbers and words of encouragement from them. I wouldn't have cared before, let alone wasted paper and pen on these people's viewpoints, but now they were newfound treasures. The final page prior to the current day's entry was a note referencing God and the St. Francis Prayer. As I wiped the tears from under my sunglasses I felt warmth, a connection to God, and gratitude that validated my renovations of value and vision.

Gratitude is not something you try to feel or a list you may make. In my opinion, gratitude comes as a gift from above, to a realization of the blessings in your life that almost overwhelm you emotionally to the point that they are a gift Divine and almost beyond your deserving. What I used to value and seek was simply ego fodder that leveraged my spiritual disconnection until I was finally able to surrender and realign with the greater intention for me.

I realize I am not important, but I can have importance. I realized I spent so much time running from my past, and I spent so much time seeking an ever-elusive sense of worth filled with an abundance of things and chasing titles. I chased personal and business connections to feel whole. I missed realizing I had all I ever needed.

When I reflected that all I wanted or needed was a clock radio, it helped me witness gratitude. I have now the same items, perhaps even less, but now I now know true wealth is in relationships; with yourself, your spirituality, your loved ones, and other living beings. Everything else is fleeting or unnecessary.

I got my coffee and drove home. I was more awake, energized, grateful, and smiling. I still have that clock radio and every time I peer at its digital face, it tells me not only the time, but to always count my blessings.

I remember most the gratitude I felt in recognizing this message. It made it clear that I was to never forget this lesson about what is of "true value." My eyes are genuinely opened wider so that I can appreciate each and every moment in the opportunities that are in front of me and were often overlooked. I have said many times, "If we miss the message, God can, and will get our attention."

I had to lay my health, relationships, and all else that I held dear on the line before I was allowed to see. I still have that black book as a reminder of my shift from ego, being stripped, and surrendering in my journey to a new place. I know I can still strive and put effort into my endeavors, but I need to maintain a connection with my priorities. When I reflect to the moment when I wrote "clock radio" in that book, I realize how disconnected I had become and how my ego was running my life. I saw too, how in a handful of hours my entire value system could be challenged. It is also these distinct moments which have become benchmarks in my growth. They are places I will always remember and value, yet never desire to return to. I am truly grateful to have traveled the path described here, and for the awareness and hierarchy of my current priorities.

Reflections

What do I truly value?

Where do I find joy?

What would happen to me in the absence of these things?

What makes me truly thankful and happy aside from other people or material things?

Can I reflect on times when I felt true gratitude?

Can I remember a time or circumstance that deeply changed who I am or how I think?

How am I better now because of it?

How can I share this experience with others to help them in a similar situation?

Poolside

It is best to be where you are when you are there!

This essay is one that truly shows my awareness of the benefits of being present. As I repeatedly read this installment, I remember how this moment in time touched me and that I did not want to it pass without sharing. I notice also, that I started to see the fruits of a new way of thinking. I was in a situation where I used to not be able to find joy or peace; this also being a situation where a lot of people typically find joy and relaxation. By being able to still my mind, I eventually did find what I was looking for.

I not only view things differently, but am able to actually feel things differently. I also see how the physical experience changes when the mind is able to embrace it as being positive and frame it in a new context. I never was one for pools and sun as an adult and had difficulty finding the enjoyment of being wet and hot, yet as a child swimming was one of my favorite pastimes. The pool didn't change, I did. I simply made the decision to change back.

I am amazed at how profound a simple choice of viewpoint placed upon normal circumstances can help achieve serenity, as opposed to irritation and disruption. I spent many years with the perspective that my sense of self-worth and my identity had a direct correlation to what I did, and what people thought of me. I had a career that placed me in a small degree of contact with the public and eventually added a small amount of media exposure to the mix.

I spent many days trying to figure out how to get ahead, and I had the mantra: "I never want anyone to be better than me, because that is a level I have not yet reached, but someone is always better, so I must always keep reaching."

It sickens me now to think I believed this to my core. That statement shows much of the egocentric insanity I participated in. It shows I had to be number one, achievement was elusive, I needed to strive to be happy, and I judged myself against the standards of others. It was self-perpetuating; pretty much my life in a nutshell.

I made a living in the beauty industry the majority of my life and did indeed have a great level of success. My nature thrived in the belief that I could make a living and make people happy at the same time. I considered my craft a gift, but one of power that stroked my ego by stroking others'. My career took me around the world, placed me on stage, television, and in print. Still it was never enough. I always felt there was another level or place I belonged and it was not here, and here did not understand me.

I often looked over my shoulder with regret thinking, "If only I would have done XYZ, I would be closer to that place, that *providence*. I often looked to the future with fear and dread. I knew some force was waiting up ahead, to laugh at me saying that I made a wrong turn years ago. *Now* was just the transition from the past to the future and nothing more. *Now* was filled with static, restlessness, and discontent. The past was still too close and the future still too far. Harmony was for losers who accepted failure too early. Those thoughts reflected my life's moral compass.

I remorsefully reflect on many blessings I could have experienced that appeared in the form of events, environments, and experiences that were lost upon me due to me not being able to be where I was when I was there. For example, when on vacation, I would dread the flight home, or worry about possible sunburn on me or my kids, sand in my shorts, the vacation being too long, too short, too boring, or too exciting to where I would dread my leaving that much more. At work while waiting to leave for vacation, I would worry about spending money I didn't have, losing clients, or perhaps them going to someone else and liking them more. I always felt I was going to miss something, like my favorite band was going to show up at the barbecue I didn't attend with supermodels and free beer. I realize now upon my study of my life, that life itself, at least for me, has a current. A current I mustn't resist.

I spent many years with my spiritual limbs exhausted by either pedaling away from my past, toward the future, or trying to control the direction intended for me. I always thought, "God has a sense of humor and I must be the punch line." I wasted a lot of time emotionally and physically avoiding now. I traded the present for projection, and attempted control of the uncontrollable. I was good at going from zero to "Armageddon." In most any situation, I could take anything, direct it at myself, and make it horrible, thereby instantaneously creating spiritual cancer for myself.

I have since learned a couple things. First, the past is dead and gone and no longer real to me. I realize I am always smarter now than I was before, either by default or by lessons learned. *Now* is the only reality I have and is where blessings, life, and gratitude lie. Also, the future is not real and has yet to be created. If I am going to create a future in my mind, I can go one of two ways. I can choose to paint an unreal picture of doom, chaos, and destruction, or I can envision a future of blessings, abundance, and happiness—although neither is real. But, if I must choose, which non-reality is more pleasurable to focus upon? Past = dead, future = not yet here, now = real. I choose to invest in now. It is hard to soar today, when my anchor is dropped in yesterday.

I see now the many doors I have slammed shut in my life, limiting myself, my spirituality, and the people around me. I also see it is the same life, with the same potential; mostly the same people; the same things; and the same highs, lows, loss, and abundance that was always there. I have simply made a choice to look at life with a new set of eyes. Instead of paddling against life's current, I now lean back and feel the sun, dip my toe in the water, listen, feel, and participate. I occasionally hit rapids, but I simply adjust my rudder as opposed to curse nature. I have my moments, but awareness keeps my navigation centered. Life is about progress not perfection.

As I write this, it is Memorial Day weekend. I am poolside with my son, surrounded by friends, sun, and warm misty air. I realize that not long ago, I would have seen things differently. The sun was hot and a perpetual source of melanoma. Chlorine made hair green. Kids were noisy. I was too fat to sunbathe, and I would rather be home wishing I was somewhere else or someone else, in location as well as life.

But right here, right now, as the gentle breeze blows the pages of my book, interrupting the flow of my writing, I casually brush them back and simply continue. I feel the soft wind on my toes and the hairs on my legs in the warmth of the sun that bathes me in comfort. I see kids frolicking, as parents watch them proudly and leisurely. I remember having fun at the city pool when I was a child. The occasional spray of a misguided squirt gun finds its way into my space and I feel the cool water punctuating my casual reclining. I hear laughter and joy, not noise. I am comfortable, not hot. I feel grateful for quality time well spent, not dreading another couple hours closer to skin cancer.

It is the same Memorial Day opportunity I have had for forty-four years, but today I have made the choice to be thankful and the choice to sense it. I made the choice to be poolside; not in the self-created depths of self-pity. Each day, even if the tasks and circumstances are similar, is a chance to experience life. I choose to stay here—now and present. I no longer curse what is any more than I curse the road I travel upon for curving left or right. I now have *life* in my lifestyle.

My final thought is: nothing in excess is healthy, including writing. It's time to join my son in the water again, and for the first time.

I remember sitting in the lawn chair and watching my son splash and play in the pool thinking, "You know, this isn't so bad; I actually kind of like this. What was I thinking?" Which is true, what was I thinking? I see how my practice of projecting ahead, making assumptions that something was going to be uncomfortable or not pleasurable usually proved me right upon my arrival to the place or situation. Now I simply decide to wait to get where I am going before I decide to label it.

I notice that staying present and connected allows me to enjoy the moments in my life more than ever before. I try to experience things with as many of my senses as possible. It allows my thoughts and five senses to connect—six opportunities to experience the true beauty in any situation. When I take the time to appreciate, or to simply seek appreciation, I often find it as easily as I could find the fault in someone or something. I also see that after years of seeking fault or failure, or waiting for the other shoe to drop; the small places and faces appear new, exciting, and fresh with my new set of eyes. As I stated in the essay, I get to do things I have done before, but again for the very first time.

Reflections

Have my preconceived assumptions of situations prohibited me from enjoying what many others find pleasurable?

Can I let go of my thoughts and connect physically with all of my senses?

Does my opinion of someone or something change when I make no prior assumptions?

Is being present and in-the-moment a challenge for me?

When I have trouble being present, where am I?

Is what consumes me real? (Past, now, future)

Do I feel any physical or emotional benefits or suffering by thinking beyond right now?

Do the past and/or future haunt me or give me hope?

The Calling

Excellence shouldn't be measured by effort and skill, but rather by the *intention* behind it.

*I always thought when someone mentioned something being his or her "calling"; it was something they were simply good at. It was a validation of the success of their efforts. I remember I was fielding questions of what I truly wanted to do or become; questions about what inspired me. Most of this was during moments I felt unrest in my career or life. I was breaking away from what was expected of me. I had always leaned toward doing or saying things that gave me approval. Now I was listening, but to a different Source. When I turned inward to listen to my heart, and I mean to **really** listen, I finally understood what people described as a calling. It is more like a call to action, a wake-up call, or a call to come home. This was the awakening of my perception of what a calling is, at least for me.*

My calling is like a lighthouse in the fog, something that keeps my navigation true and me safe in traveling toward my destination. My calling is not a specific trade or activity or action, rather it is the essence of me that allows me to connect wholly to what it is I am here on earth to accomplish. It is the synchronization of my dreams, personal fulfillment, and Divine intention.

Until recently, I was under the mistaken impression that one's calling was simplified in description by being one's personal fulfillment in a task he or she performed. It was what allowed the performer to feel correctly connected to what he or she was meant to *do*. I also correlated that when people were steeped in their calling, they were successful, happy, and abundantly blessed; that they had arrived.

I always thought I had found my calling. I am a hairstylist and, by the grace of God, have been successful. I have been blessed to have traveled the world, taught many, and have been a mentor, leader, and a speaker. My work has and does appear regularly in local, national, and international magazines. I also appeared frequently on local television and radio. I own a salon that has bottles of great hair-care products with my name on the labels lining its shelves. I am very lucky, blessed, and thankful. I, and others, would say that I was someone who had found his calling. This may be untrue.

As my blessings and things continued to escalate and accumulate, I always felt "a disturbance in the force" if you will. It felt like something wasn't quite correct. Not necessarily wrong, but like a good shot that was just off the bull's-eye. I spent many, many hours, years even, wondering what I was or wasn't doing correctly. I felt my compass was always off. Yes, I was somewhat successful, not rich, but successful as I truly believe abundance comes to those traveling down the correct path. I also felt that passion provided eventually. Every time a door opened, or I got a title or promotion, or when I connected with someone important, it validated my path and secured another rung of progress toward my calling. Things were going well. "I must be doing something right," I thought.

I also experienced pitfalls and valleys. I believed the harder you fall, the higher you can bounce, and bounce I would. I experienced family estrangement, lost money, lost fame, lost favor, ended up in a treatment center, and sat in psychologists' chairs—and have recovered apparently well each time. This proved to me that I must have been fulfilling my calling. To lead, own a business, be visible in the community, gain abundance, receive "attaboys" from friends and loved ones, and write my memoirs in the sun during the middle years of my life—well, after all that, "Why am I feeling this void," I thought. Why the feeling of being left onshore while my ship is sailing? Am I the most shallow, selfish, egocentric person who is incapable of finding serenity in his blessings, when others suffer? Perhaps.

As I reflect, I am happy, but feel that I have more to give. That is when it hit me. It is not what I need to *get*, but what I desire to *give*. I do have more than enough. If I never gained another dollar, toy, home, or car, I would be okay, and my spirit or happiness would never need to suffer. My spirit, on the other hand, has wings that need to soar upon the winds of helping others, and needs to share hope and love as I have experienced.

Recently, when I was asked about my "gifts," I started to explore this new path. I did not want to limit myself by only identifying what I *did*, as I thought giving a good haircut and refreshing banter was not all I had in me. So, I looked deeper. I realized I have an intuition that allows me to adapt and connect with people from many walks of life. I am blessed with understanding without prejudice, a love for all, and a desire to learn about others as it can only enrich me. I also have the ability to see commonality in seemingly different entities and people, and can create connection among them. Finally, I love to inspire and inform by sharing my knowledge and experiences, to not impose, but rather to allow the observer to "absorb what is useful, reject what is useless, and add specifically what is their own" (to quote Bruce Lee). I also realize when these forces and activities occur within and around me I am most in tune, connected, and present.

Calling for me is *presence with purpose*. It is where I am aware of what state I am in, and causes a sense of purpose I feel that is divinely inspired. When I am being called, it is like being pulled toward something with a cosmic attraction, as opposed to me trying to achieve it. I also find when I am being impatient or unfulfilled; I am causing my ego to seek, as opposed to my soul drifting in the current of my calling. I have to remember that progress can be as subtle as the movement of a glacier, or as powerful as the thrust of a tsunami. This pace can and will fluctuate frequently, and I know now that it is correct and true. Progress, no matter how unnoticeable, is still progress. Progress is evolving and allows the journey to remain in an inspiring state. The pauses and delays allow time for reflection as well as appreciation.

To find my calling, I decided to stop seeking what I was to *do* and instead concentrate on what gave me *fulfillment* and a sense of *connection*. It was about emotional, not material, attachment or attainment. It was about looking for an essence — a state, and not to a title, task, or achievement. When you find your calling, the path may eventually bring elevation in some degree of status, or financial abundance, or friends and connections—not that it is sought, but as a by-product of the peace of being true to your nature and internal desire; that your spirituality is stimulated and your core is inspired. I believe there is magnetism to those with the peace of being where they are supposed to be. All are aligned in the same current.

I also feel a true calling has an element of service to others. I believe that when people follow their calling, there is a transfer of energy and love that is equally beneficial to the giver and the receiver. When I share and when I serve, I am frequently shared with and served as well; often times tenfold over.

I realize my calling is not what I *do*; rather it is a *state* I wish to achieve. If I stay present and connected with my calling, I will be aware of when I allow my ego to take over, and when I let others infiltrate and defeat me, and create false excuses. I can also see progress, no matter how momentary, miniscule, or monumental. My thoughts, words, and deeds will propel me in the current of my calling. I know that what I do is not always in correlation to what my calling is or to how I service my fellow man, regardless if I am in a service career. I now dedicate my conscious efforts toward connecting and responding to this current.

We often find reasons why we cannot follow the pull, our instinct, or our calling. Usually it is a threatened ego trying to remain intact. When doubt enters, defenses emerge. We must focus on the peace we feel when we know we are connected to our passion. We must revel in our newfound sense of purpose and direction. Becoming present and remembering all thoughts and deeds we do now are progress toward our calling. Remember also that God's delays are not necessarily God's denials. No one can feel our internal passion. For the people on the outside, it is easy to negate the path and passions of others. Others will often criticize those who answer this calling as being foolish or impulsive. No one can defeat us, unless we allow him or her to do so.

I hope the energy I had when writing this essay was sensed. It was like I had a treasure map and finally saw the big X marking where the pirates buried the treasure. When aligned with our calling, we move beyond motivation to inspiration, where our drive inside becomes much deeper and more spiritual.

For me, I can sense that what I am called to do is correct, and any detours will still allow me to arrive at the determined destination. I realize that looking for a career or endeavor will not necessarily connect you to your calling in all cases. For example, I am called to connect with others through communication; to inspire others through the verbal and visual. Perhaps this is why I have been fortunate in the arts, media and writing. When I found the most important part of my calling, "for the good of others," is when I realized the skills I had are to be of service to my fellow man. Instantaneously, life seemed right. It was like I was finally going home and that my Creator was going to show me the way. It felt like a fire and a peace simultaneously. Once I surrendered to my calling, many serendipitous events started to unfold—you reading this book is the result of one of those events.

Reflections

Have I ever felt there was something more for me; like my skill or energy was still untapped?

Am I drawn to an activity or place, even though it has nothing to do with my current lifestyle?

What are my true inner strengths are and how can I use them to better my life and serve others?

Do I believe I am truly doing what I am supposed to be doing in this life?

If I could choose to do or be anything (let's say money is no object), am I doing it?

If not, can what obstacles are holding me back?

Are those obstacles truths or fears?

Race Car Driver

Not only do we often create our own chaos, we are usually in a hurry to get the job done!

I had a little fun here. Mainly because I could see where I was compared to where I am now. I find some of my previous states laughable, especially when I realize how much irritation I endured, and yet could have made it disappear instantaneously. This essay is about self-inflicted pain or insanity, and to me is, and was, a very big eye-opener. I tried to share some humor, and it is only because I now get it—or at least am aware when my state shifts.

I am thankful to realize the interesting paradox of how people try to avoid discomfort, conflict, and confrontation; yet we often become our own biggest perpetrators and aggressors. We take ourselves to places we fear most—to places where we are out of control, or unaware, and even self-destructive. I have also found that this mindset will continually morph and seek holes in our defenses if we do not train ourselves to be aware when we proceed down this slippery slope. For me, stories like this one can help me remember to practice, or to avoid certain behaviors, like remembering a moral or a parable with a message. Let's see if you can identify with this one in any way.

While going about my day-to-day activities I am reminded of things I am grateful for. I am given the opportunity to enjoy where I am now as opposed to where I was. I also appreciate reflecting upon jobs I have had, relationships current and lost, and a laundry list of things I once valued that are no longer important. One day, as I was driving to work, I remembered I used to be a race car driver.

I consider myself blessed with the ability to appreciate the past, the good and bad, the exciting and mundane, as being part of the building blocks of who I am. My racing days are no exception. Every morning I would mentally prepare myself with the strategies I was going to need to complete the race: speed, fuel, timing, and an aggressive competitive demeanor to name a few. I could not settle for number two, even though I knew there were others who were going to do what it took to put me in my place, taking my position, and trying to crush my spirit and take the cup from me. As soon as I left the house, I was in the zone. I entered the car with a calm that soon would be devoured by the competitive moment. Dressed, ready, and all systems go, I entered the raceway assessing the competition. The green light would open the way for the slow and inattentive to be overtaken by the focused and fast. Driving was a game of chess. I had to be aware of where I was and think ahead. I knew I could be cut off at any second, disrespected and discouraged, and lose valuable position, which simply was not an option.

I rarely noticed the beauty of the tracks I raced on, as my vision was locked on the cars in front of me. Subtle changes of speed or braking could easily pinch out the car next to me and a simple feeling of satisfaction would come to me as I maintained my lane and position. I didn't care if I bent the rules or placed myself in peril—that was how the game was played. You get there fast, and you get there first!

The other drivers were not my friends. It was me and only me, and the road was mine all mine. I owned the track was going to school anyone with the desire to debate, and debate they did.

As I reflect now, I realize I never won a race. I am also glad now that I have retired to the slow lane. I often would arrive in good time in the best position, but still never won. I never ever got a trophy. I would often exit my car either frustrated, angry, and heart pounding, still never experiencing the thrill of victory. I never received hugs or adoration for the swift maneuvers of cutting off the other guy and speeding past. There was no victory laps, no photo circles, nothing valuable gained. It wasn't because I didn't spend enough time thinking about the race, it wasn't because I did not drive aggressively enough, as I would white knuckle it from the time I entered the car until my exit. It also wasn't because I didn't take risks, because I often came within inches from causing a collision. It was simply this: there was no race.

I spent much of my life competing and trying to win contests, feats, and competitions that were only conjured in my mind. Someone was out to get me, take what was mine, or better me in life's game. My ego was in constant control, and I was not going to come in second, in anything, ever!

As I was driving to work the other day, I was lucky to see a race, but this time I had nothing invested. I was very close to the race, maybe even considered by others a participant, and if I was, I would be more of a pace car now; slow, steady, and not working to win. I saw three vehicles—an SUV, a service repair truck, and a midsized sports car—apparently all of them noticed simultaneously that the two lanes ahead were merging into one. The light turned green, and they were off!

The sports car jockeyed for position and was closing in on the bumper of the SUV because it was not moving fast enough. The sports car swerved in the lane, looking for an opportunity to take over the second-place slot. In an instant, the service truck, in a daring feat, pulled left into the lane that was merging into the other, just barely missing the bumper of the SUV, then swung right and took the lead, only to slam on its brakes because of a red light that caused all three to stop suddenly. I was not impeded, as there was a turn lane I pulled into, with no one in front of me. Before turning and calmly continuing my journey, I looked at the racers from the "sideline."

The guy in the sports car was talking to himself in frustration, the lady in the SUV in front of him seemed concerned to be sandwiched closely by two strange vehicles, and the *winner* was talking and gesturing rudely into his rearview mirror. I doubt they had met prior to that brief moment, yet each now the other's nemesis. I have been all three characters in the past. If they had been me, I suspect the losing drivers will carry the resentments created from the race all day. I know I would.

I remembered races I had that resulted in getting my car punched, loud cursing, weapons being brandished, and other disturbing circumstances. I now know that I can choose to enter or exit a race at will. I can enter that self-created competitive ego state or I can stay in the pace car, slow and steady, pulling off the track when things get heavy. I arrive at my destinations serene, happy, and safe. I don't even know what to do with my middle finger anymore.

Maybe sometime I will share stories of when I was a real estate mogul, as yes, I did own the whole road. I also owned many parking lots where people would take *my* spot. Also many did not know *who I was*, and my *importance*, otherwise the line in the grocery would move faster. I was also amazed how easily people lost their ability to read minds, especially mine, to know when I needed my drink refilled in a restaurant, when I deserved a raise, when I needed affection, my needs, my needs, my needs.

It is so nice to participate in the "what is is" mindset. To stay present and enjoy the ride and to find peace and humor in life's trivial happenings is a blessing. So much less passes me by, and I have such sensory connection, gratitude, and acceptance over that which used to cripple and consume me. I am not saying I am free of my character defects, heavens no. I just now have an awareness that can intercept the madness sooner. I can choose humanity or insanity. I can interrupt my past desires to "race" by asking myself, "What is the prize for first place?" The answer is, "Probable frustration and a possible heart attack!"

After writing this and practicing awareness, I have noticed patience, acceptance, and peace are the by-products of this practice. It can laugh now, but I also sadly reflect on how I would participate, disarming myself, and hold onto the anger for a length of time far beyond the incident. So much was wrong with me; my ego, my soul, my patience, my acceptance, and my ability to be present, all crippled by my own doing. I now own all this madness I subjected myself to. I no longer feel people woke up early, waited on me at an intersection, pulled out in front of me, and decided to drive four miles below the speed limit to see if I would have a stroke over it. I used to feel victimized and take life's random speed bumps so personally.

Now I decide whether or not the circumstance warrants my attention or power. Is it strong enough to disarm me? Is the red light, person in front of me in line at the grocery store with coupons, spilled glass of milk, dog doo, late client, angry gesture or comment, weeds in the garden, or a hard rain enough to take me down? They are what they are, and will continue to be. I realize that my state and awareness is a shield against the times my ego enters me in a race I do not want to be in. To reiterate, there is no prize for first place, except maybe hair loss, high blood pressure, indigestion, or a satin-lined casket.

Reflections

Did I identify with any of the points in this essay; if yes, which ones.

Do I get upset easily? Do other people frustrate me?

Would I be happier if things went my way?

Do I feel victimized or like I am a target?

Are there simple life adjustments I can make to reduce my stress? (I.e. leave earlier, take a different route, and examine someone else's viewpoint?)

Do I carry the stress of a situation far beyond when I encountered it?

Sometimes is it my *perception* of a situation and not the *reality* that upsets me?

Am I willing to take ownership when certain situations occur and I overreact?

It's Not Just For Sundays Anymore

We all hear Heaven's music with different ears.

*My current quest is to seek connection and understanding in my faith and to bond with compassion leveraged by something Divine. In the past, I used a variety of belief systems as platforms of **exclusion** rather than **inclusion**. The incident I write of sparked awareness of when I judge others, and often unfairly. It was a lesson in opening my mind to different perspectives and ideas. I realize I do not have to agree to, absorb, or practice things I encounter. However, I can show love and understanding regardless of the encounter—which does not have to be considered an endorsement.*

The night was coming to a close as my wife, son, and I were leaving a pleasant party celebrating a friend's birthday. The evening consisted of a potluck of creations lovingly served to allow friends and family to enjoy shared recipes both current, and passed down through generations. Music, the laughter of children, and light, friendly banter became the soundtrack of the evening. I enjoyed the company set in the cradle of the surrounding trees and well-manicured landscaping.

My night was spent appreciating our surroundings, even prompting me to upload a photo from my chair to share with friends on a popular online social network. I was also entertained by a precocious two-year-old little girl, a daughter of a friend sharing in innocent games of peek-a-boo. This routine was only interrupted by my own daughter Alexa, and her friends coming over to visit. Questions of playground rivalries, boys, bras, embarrassment, and other amusing stories a 10-year-old daughter would feel comfortable sharing with her daddy were the platform. As Alexa sat on my lap, rubbing my arm, seemingly enjoying my company as much as that of her friends, I reveled in the fact that she and her friends would share their time with me.

After a beautiful evening with friends it eventually became time for our departure. My daughter opted for a sleepover with friends, and my son retired to his booster seat in the back of our SUV joined by my wife for a rare ride in the backseat of our own car. She agreed to at the request of our son.

I love today's technology, especially when it comes to music. No longer must I rummage through random cassettes and CDs trying to find a particular favorite song or playlist. With the use of my MP3 player and, better yet, my favorite website that allows my phone to become a virtual DJ, I can create a self-made mix of ambient music to go with any job, task, or experience with the simple click of a mouse. I frequently make soundtracks to enhance the mood of any endeavor, including, but not limited to: mowing the yard, driving, cooking and entertaining.

As I was driving my wife and son home, I turned on a selection called "morning mix," which I created as a nice background mix when I cooked and served breakfast to my wife and a close friend of hers one Sunday morning. It had become a favorite of mine. It was a compilation of acoustic versions of my favorite songs, some old, some new, and some obscure. The melodic state, in which the tempo of the songs and the mood fluctuated gently, kept you engaged but not overly focused. I had practically worn this CD out and found it equally enjoyable for evening driving as well. This became the chosen soundtrack for our drive home that evening. The night was crisp from the upcoming thunderstorm, the air was warm, and since it was the end of a nice night it seemed the perfect background for our brief journey.

About three songs in, my wife, who I thought was asleep, broke the silence of our conversation and asked if the music was from a "Christian" CD. I was taken aback and performed a quick mental inventory of the music trying to justify her question. The music had soft melody, spiritual connotations, and references to perhaps praying and connection, but it truly was not Christian; at least not under any current Christian label. I felt it was definitely secular in nature. I stated, "It is not Christian. I guess it could be considered *spiritual*, but it was not intended either way." After a brief pause she asked, "Do you have a problem with God?" To which I responded, "Absolutely not! I feel more connected than I ever have in my life!" That was it; we ventured onward to our destination, arriving home safely.

This brief exchange lingered with me. I recapped it during my late-morning shower the following day, a Sunday. I don't have a problem with God or people's personal choice of expression at all; period! I love all believers or non-believers, those who question and those who are convinced. I find it bold for anyone to challenge another person's belief and, therefore, I respect that others can differ and disagree with me.

I do believe that eventually truth will be revealed, and we will somehow be held accountable in some way for our life path and belief systems; somehow. Also personal interpretations vary. Let me simplify, as an interpretation of a Supreme Being is too difficult for some to either identify with or even bring into a descriptive visual manifestation, let's look at a tree. If I asked everyone to paint a picture of a tree, and we did so, then we compared pictures, they would most likely be a recognizable tree, but whose tree is correct? I believe that many who believe in a Supreme Being has a vision of their Creator ranging from a grandfatherly old man in beautiful robes, to an enchanting voice with that of a likeness to James Earl Jones, to a consciousness that speaks to them, and so on. It is how they personally connect, and the key word is "personally".

Let's take a moment again to talk about the tree. Now perhaps the discussion among tree drawings would turn to how many leaves should it have, what color should it be, how tall, how grand, the bark, the roots, and so on. What I find is that the focus then shifts to the personal *mental image* as opposed to the *quality of the connection* to what the image represents. I have people in my life who have either spent their life searching for meaning in trying to find a place to settle into, and how to be able to connect with their Creator. Many will connect with their Creator through books, fellowship, and brick-and-mortar structures. It is a blessing and a testimony to the importance of this connection by the proliferation of these resources, and they are quite valuable to maintain a spiritual relationship. The *way* one connects is a personal choice and I hope it brings them closer to that which they seek as it has done for me.

I think it was my ego that got to me that night. My wife's question about the genre of the music I played led me to question my faith and caused me to react in a way I am not proud of, one of supremacy and "my beliefs are correct!" They are not as *correct* as they are *personal*.

I know from where my blessings rise; I attend "church" daily and pray and give thanks often. I realize that faith is in the heart and I can stay spiritually connected by choice, whenever and wherever a lesson is imposed on me. The greatest insight, connection, and gratitude—"hugs from heaven"—come to me from sources that range from biblical to the obscure, but I never dismiss one or another as being any less divine. I have my receptors turned on 24/7; not exclusively in an allocated building, in front of a designated person, or at any specified day or time. The randomness and impact can hit me like a butterfly landing or a stray bullet; they vary in nature and are enduring for me. I respect all sources and do not dismiss any one as being more or less important, sacred, or divine.

I see now the dialogue between my wife and me that evening was poignant for me. My ego intercepted my thoughts that night. I also realize I am not a fan of labels when discussing from where my inspiration is derived, such as *spiritual, Christian, good, bad, right, wrong,* etc. Labels are personal and relative. I wonder if when my wife asked if the music was Christian, if she was feeling a connection, or maybe receiving her own message, having a spiritual moment, or getting a nudge from God. I don't know, and it was hers to own and to decide. What I know is that moment enriched me, and the next time I am asked if the music is Christian, I will either be silent or respond, "It is if you need it to be."

The quest to understand another's point of view shows love, respect, compassion, and acceptance of the individual; it is not an endorsement or participation in their belief system. I believe that is what our Creator expects.

Divine insight, connection, as well as spiritual, and life-changing experiences can happen anytime, anywhere. They can absolutely happen in designated locations, like churches, temples, and synagogues; but they can also occur when you are alone or in the presence of another, and they can be tangible or intangible. They come as lessons in the best form for us to receive them, at the time we are supposed to receive them. I find the deepest spiritual gifts and messages I have received have come to me in the most obscure places, *in the form of song, quotes, or visual manifestations, in the exact place where I am **supposed** to see them.*

My simple request is to not limit your scope; to be open to new places and to see things that might have been under your nose for a long time. Sometimes lessons are presented in a classroom we were not even aware we were sitting in. Daily life can also be "church" and there is always an empty pew beckoning with messages of love, gratitude, and hope.

Reflections

Do I judge others because their beliefs differ from mine?

Do I think my beliefs are the *best* beliefs, or the *only* beliefs?

Can I respect others for what they believe?

Have I ever been spiritually or deeply touched by an odd or unique situation?

Can I only be connected to something greater while in a place of worship or with a certain book or other item?

What inspires me or makes me feel introspective or emotional on a spiritual level?

Can I share these things or do I keep them private because I believe others will find them strange or unusual?

If I understood certain people or beliefs better, could I at least accept them and eliminate judgment?

The Storm

Sometimes it is our storms that show us where our leaks are!

Ever notice how one event or a single statement, no matter how benign, can sometimes be taken the wrong way, and thereby have a catastrophic effect on your mental well-being? It is like being on a runaway chariot with no reins to guide the horses. Once this happens, other minor and completely unrelated issues can fuel this mindset with compound interest.

For me, it used to be very difficult to get a hold of "it," before "it" got a hold of me and then take me to an ego wonderland for an undetermined amount of time. What helps me now is practicing awareness, so that my ego can't get the best of me and totally fog my reality and subsequently my perception of what is happening, and how I feel about it.

Awareness, in and of itself, takes just enough energy away from the negative situation, allowing me to escape. Then, I direct my attention to something pleasant and focus on it in as much detail as possible to momentarily disconnect myself from that which disarms me. This starts to bring me to presence in the now, which pulls the reins on the runaway chariot. It gives me a chance to reestablish control and navigate the situation in a more positive and healthy way. Through this practice of reestablishing presence, I can start my day over at any time I need to, no matter what the clock says.

One day I did the math. As a member of a popular social networking website, I was often greeted on Monday mornings with recaps of weekends, "off to work" updates, and reasons people loathed Mondays. My job allows me to have Mondays free from a normal work schedule. I just often tend to random tasks and errands that I can schedule to accommodate my whims and needs. Typically Mondays are benign to me. My wife and son stay home, my daughter goes to school, so most often they are almost an extension of Sundays for me. I never bought into the "I don't like Mondays" brigade, even when supported by the song made popular by Bob Geldof. I found any day could pose its challenges, and Mondays also were like a reset button on a chance to have a good week.

One day, in response to a friend's posting of "I hate Mondays", I felt prompted to calculate something. If a person lived to around eighty-ish, and hated Mondays, he or she would be spending approximately eleven years of their life in dread or a state of hatred. Should they choose to add yet another day, well, you can do the math. It just seems foolish to me. This simple observation allowed me to avoid projecting my ill-will, and to disconnect from any negative feelings I may try to place upon the innocent start of the week. Not a healthy way to start a week, nor end a weekend.

If I don't stay present and aware, my ego can sneak in the back door and take my mind hostage for a while. At times, it has even been like throwing a blanket over it, beating it with a club, throwing in the trunk of a car, and driving out to the country and throwing it in a ditch only to emerge wondering "what the *bleep* just happened?"

I find using tools for staying present and to connect to what is happening right now are crucial to my sanity and peace. I make it a practice to try to stay aware and alert and to not let the "mental termites" eat away at me and cause structural spiritual damage. I have become better, not perfect. The Monday I write this the "termites" got me. Kind of like that alien bug Khan inserted into the ears of his captured Starship Enterprise enemies in the movie *Star Trek: The Wrath of Khan*. (I apologize if you're unfamiliar with the *Star Trek* reference. Those who do get it will appreciate it.)

The first of the month fell on a Monday following a wonderful weekend. Every first of the month I am greeted by a reminder on my computer that I owe thousands of dollars to random people for my business obligations. The timing of the start of the month, money due, impending rain, and a less-than-perfect night's sleep left me in a fragile state. I still managed to complete my daily duties. I was up at 7:00 a.m., got my daughter off to school, watched a bit of news on TV, drank some coffee, and then moved onto the day's business tasks. I checked e-mail and bank balances, drank more coffee, looked at the weather forecast, read my horoscope, and let the dog outside. The usual routines were blah, but not that bad.

Since my wife and son are also home on Mondays, we have to discuss and coordinate our personal schedules to determine which one of us is going to be home for the kids, which often means determining whose schedule is "more important." That morning a debate ensued, followed by my resentments and a lack of resolution.

I still went about my day. I went to the bank, and the post office, and also ran an errand for my wife. I had groceries to get and I still needed to mow, and was going to help a friend with some of her career issues later. The house was messy, there were things to do, the rain was coming, and it was just going to be a rough day I thought. How *dare* my wife question where I was going and for how long? I mean, really! I had *tons* to do and the errands would keep me busy *all* morning (they only took twenty minutes), rain was *surely* going to interrupt my morning, and what other day could I possibly find time to do yard work? On top of that, the kids left balls in the yard! Can you believe it?! Kids?! Balls?! (They took all of thirty seconds to gather and fling onto their trampoline.)

I ran the errands, including doing one for my wife thinking that the simple gesture would shift my mental gears and get me out of my own head. Instead, it simply reminded me that the errand was *out of my way* and eventually I returned home to a soft rumble of thunder. "C'mon!!" I thought exasperated, as I still had to mow, and then had to leave to help my friend later. I thought that if it rained, it would surely be another couple of days before I would get to it, thus postponing this hectic schedule until later. (Our yard takes 45 minutes *tops* to mow, including start up, bagging, and cleanup.)

I put away the balls as well as two lawn chairs "irresponsibly" left in the yard. "Lawn chairs don't belong in the yard!" I angrily muttered as I drug them onto the patio. The skies were darkening and the distant thunder increased in frequency and volume. I started the mower, grabbed a yard waste bag, and ventured outward toward the front lawn, scurrying down the driveway hoping to at least get part of the front mowed before it was too wet. "Well, if *she* wanted the yard mowed so badly, *she* could have done it. *I* wanted to do it yesterday, but noooo, we had to spend a *family* day at the pool!" I bitterly thought feeling sorry for myself.

The droning of the mower was the ambient background for my incessant grumbling as I proceeded mowing the lawn. I opted for the parallel line pattern instead of the diagonal. My wife likes the diagonal, I like the quick. Rain today, and so quick it is.

The air was getting crisp, as it often does prior to rain, and I pushed the mower faster than its self-propulsion unit would allow, soon finding myself out of breath. The rain was not going to beat me. I was now the martyr, with all the errands and mowing soon completed. A hero's welcome awaited me. If I wasn't too exhausted, I would acquire a week's groceries to insure I earned my Superman cape.

I usually enjoy mowing the yard, as it is easy and pleasantly landscaped; a nice time for reflection and solitude. Today the rain challenged me to a race and I was also "spite-mowing" at my wife, and I knew I was not going to get everything done or have time to relax. Eventually, the front and back were mowed and looking pristine. The mower was returned to the garage. I may have even shaved five minutes off the time. I would have to check to see if my strife and efforts paid off.

The rain started at the exact moment I returned to the threshold of the garage door to close it. I noticed the rain starting by the telltale dark, irregular dime-sized circles starting to appear on the dusty blacktop. "Victory", I smugly thought—but the feeling was immediately erased, like when you shake an Etch-a-Sketch to get rid of an improperly created image. My morning insanity had left. Something *beyond me* facilitated the detachment from my anger and released the pressure gauge, thus allowing the beginning of the emotional de-escalation to occur.

I love rain, thunder, lightning, and all that goes with the marvelous conscious witness of a good spring rain. Nothing torrential, but a good show of nature in its cleansing state is always a welcome reprieve. I found myself smiling when I realized the laundry list of tasks that were taxing my ability to stay present and at peace, the long serenity-crippling list of duties that were destined to *ruin my day*, were completed by 10:45 a.m.

It was those damn "mental termites" again! I casually ambled up the driveway and decided as the rain had increased to just chill out on our front step. I was about three feet shy of the protection of our porch's cover. I just sat and observed, connected, and listened.

I have always been a fan of rain showers and even appreciated CDs and radios with nature sounds as an alternative, but nothing compares to nature's spontaneous gifts. I first noticed the droplets hitting my skin. They were cold at first, and refreshing, then evaporating to be continually replaced by yet another. At first I felt them on my exposed skin, on my arms and legs eventually turned my attention to my clothing. The droplets caused a darker color variation as they were absorbed into my clothing, and then began their disappearance. It was a tug-of-war between saturation and evaporation. It was cooling, calming, and of no concern to me how it ended.

The aromas in the air turned from crisp and clean to the initial musty smell from the environmental soot being lifted off of where it lies. The smell of the wet sidewalk is distinct and teased childhood memories out of me for some reason. The air became thick with the moisture falling from the sky and the mist mixed with the earth to release the familiar rain-soaked aroma.

At first, the patter of the droplets on welcoming leaves dry from the previous day's sun dominated. But, upon closer observation, I realized all the vegetation gave off its own percussive noises as the rain increased. It was a true symphony. The clicks escalated into a continual soothing white noise that I can only describe as nature saying "shhhhhh!" It caused me to listen even deeper. Nature's music was punctuated by the "whissshhh" of an occasional set of car tires entering then exiting the performance, as well as a barking dog begging to be let indoors.

I experienced rolling thunder that day. I have always thought thunder fascinating, but never really experienced its roll. Thunder has a voice; a deep commanding voice that communicates to the sky. I noticed bass and treble, like the arguing of a father and son vying for vocal dominance. The thunder appeared as a wave in the distance, increasing the decibels as it approached. Like a wave, it had momentum, a crescendo, and then a crash before dissipating and retreating. Like standing on a shore, I waited for the next flash of lightning to foretell of another impending wave of nature's voice.

The rain increased and danced about drumming on the leaves of my potted plants and surrounding trees, all responding with a "nod" from the touch of the droplets. The ground now blanketed with a wet glisten, and the sidewalks and pavement had puddles, giving feedback in the form of small dancing splashes. I watched as insects scurried to avoid the onslaught. The trees' seeds and the mulch flipped and changed color with the moisture's falling intensity. As I retreated passively toward more shelter, I watched as the silhouette of my derrière on the porch, which transformed from dry to damp in seconds.

It was absolute bliss. My son briefly joined me wondering why his dad lost his mind and was sitting in the rain, but upon joining me in the shelter of our porch, he sat in awe silently with me, breaking the solitude with an occasional "coooool!" in reference to a recent clap of thunder. He retreated to the house; I remained outside for a few more minutes.

The morning's folly and fury were gone. Some may call this meditation; I consider it that, but more a *reconnection*. I plugged back into the present. I find now that the most familiar things in my life and surroundings are still yet unexplored. There is so much to absorb, appreciate, and study. When I am focused on being where I am when I'm there, I avoid the ego's projections, mental disruptions, worries, and other insanity that can infiltrate my state; the termites are held at bay.

I can find the same type of connection while cooking, watching my kids play, and sitting at a barbecue, working in my garden, riding a bike, and most certainly writing. I recommend practicing reconnecting by opening all your senses and really listening to what is around you. I mean *really* listening and opening up and just breathing; just being. It can allow you a do-over at any time in your day, and I find what I experience sticks with me. The rain I experienced today was one of the most profound I have been a part of in forty-four years.

The storm passed, the sun returned, and my surroundings are fresh, clean, and energized; as is my mental state. I got a do-over. The ruined day was renewed and redeemed. I laugh at the labels I unsuccessfully tried to place on it only a few short hours ago, only to be replaced by a precious gift. I also realize the danger of the storm that appeared long before the rain.

I have used this sense of connection before in areas such as martial arts, trying to overcome or endure pain, or to simply seek introspective answers. Focusing on something positive redirects my energy, which makes it difficult to stay in an undesirable place for long. By tuning in to the present, I can activate my sensory receptors. What do I see, hear, feel, smell, taste? I try not to be a judge, but simply to recognize the moment. Abstaining from labels and judgment is the key to being present and in a positive state.

Try to simply notice and connect with how you feel. Become aware of your thoughts and mind; do not follow it in any direction. This does, indeed, require practice and it is more useful the more disruptive the situation.

Reflections

Do I have trouble with one negative thought taking me to another and then another?

Do I have trouble getting these thoughts out of my head?

Can I focus on things easily or am I easily distracted?

What are my opinions and thoughts on "being in the now" and "presence?"

Can I connect with what is around me and block out busy thoughts?

When you take these quiet moments, are you able to calm yourself? Do you find that if you return to a disturbing situation, you are better prepared to handle it?

Exercise: Try to experience what is around you. Start by spending two minutes noticing as much as you can. Remain quiet and simply breathe. How did you feel? Try expanding the amount of time you spend on this exercise.

The World Is Flat And The Sky Is Falling

Sometimes it is what we *know* that shows our true ignorance!

The two parts of the title are both belief systems that we may have encountered from fables heard in our youth. Both can be counterproductive, disruptive to ourselves and others, and may even present a sense of fear or panic.

*This essay presents my observation of things I once "knew" or believed, which showed my disregard of the truth. I acted on negative perceptions and misinformation without evaluating the source of the truths and beliefs I held onto. Oftentimes they limited my growth and ability to experience joy or pleasure and skewed my perceptions, and held me in an inactive and fearful state. I realized that sometimes I created these truths to justify or rationalize my inactivity or laziness in tackling a situation. I also used them to intellectualize and to manipulate others into joining me in my views. Perhaps I was afraid to let go. Maybe I was afraid of being wrong. I see now that **my** truth isn't necessarily the truth of everyone else.*

Knowledge is power, right? Well maybe. It depends on your definition and identification with "knowing" something. I see now "knowing" teeters between a blessing and a burden. In the past, I really would not watch news or read the paper. I didn't have to. Now I could if I wanted to just throw gas on a fire, but I could already awaken in the morning with all I would need to know for the day. Clairvoyance? No. Madness? Perhaps. Projection? Absolutely!

In the morning, I could tell you how my entire day was going to go, from start to finish upon the alert of my alarm clock. I was often tired upon awakening as I was notorious for having many "3 a.m. meetings" with myself. I would have a noisy committee of one going over what needed to be done, deeds needing tended to, potential challenging encounters, who I knew I was going to disappoint, or who would disappoint me. This meeting never had a set schedule, but the committee often showed up in the middle of the night, as the committee knew it had a captive audience. I am surprised with all the noise and chatter my wife never awoke, but the room was really silent in the midnight darkness. The noise was all in my head.

Interrupted sleep often caused me to awaken grumpy and emotionally spent, even after eight or so hours on the rack. As soon as the alarm rang, I **knew** it was going to be a rough day. I **knew** my kids were going to pose a challenge to get up. They would also be loud, and hard to get motivated. I **knew** my favorite clothes were probably dirty, as I **knew** it was my wife's fault. I **knew** my back would hurt, my feet would ache, and I **knew** traffic would be tight. I **knew** I would be late for work. I **knew** being late would make my first client upset, and I **knew** that I would surely have all of my most difficult clients. I **knew** they could be picky, and I **knew** I would be frustrated trying to please them. Worst yet, I **knew** my business would be slow, as the sands of my financial survival would be draining, mocking my efforts. Therefore, I **knew** everyone else at work would be in a bad mood. So, I **knew** I wouldn't be able to get to eat lunch soon enough, but since I **knew** I would be late in the morning, nourishment for me was in jeopardy, and I **knew** I would be stuck at work hungry. I also **knew** it would be late in the day before I would get to eat. I **knew** that I would be leaving work around rush hour to get the kids, whom I **knew** would be hungry, and since I **knew** traffic would suck, it would be that much longer until we could eat. I **knew** we had nothing at home, so I **knew** I would have to feed the kids at a restaurant. I **knew** we would never agree on which restaurant to choose, and I **knew** they would want the most expensive, probably with the worst service. I **knew** by the time dinner was over my kids would be picking at each other, and I **knew** homework and bath time were going to be a trial. I **knew** I was going to be exhausted, and I **knew** I was never going to get a chance to just sit. I **knew** when my wife came home, she would want to talk about work and I **knew** it would be bad. I **knew** she would be mad when I would decline to talk, and I **knew** when I retreated to bed for the night, I would have to make the messy bed left over from last night. I **knew** when I got into bed that my back was going to hurt, as I **knew** our bed was to blame. I **knew** I was going to have trouble sleeping. I would touch the alarm to double check the time for my morning wake-up because I **knew** I would forget to otherwise. 7:00 a.m., check! Now, I would wait to drift off only to meet up with the committee I **knew** would noisily appear in the middle of that night to taunt me. The point of this is that my alarm rang at 7:00 a.m., and the above scenario played through my mind by 7:01 a.m. Odds are, I could make all this come true in my head.

My knowing of the day's events was no more valid—but just as real—as when early man thought the world was flat. And, just like Chicken Little, I had mastered the art of worst-case scenario. I could take something quite random and process it into a catastrophe. I could turn sniffles into cancer, and my monthly bills into bankruptcy like a wizard. Not just from point A to point B, but every stop in between with all the supporting arguments to give my mind momentum and support. Why? Because I "knew" it! Where did this knowing come from? It came from my mental archives, my emotional library, in which I personally penned every volume.

This knowing enabled every fear, excuse, failure, and barrier I could find. It hindered my potential happiness. In hindsight, I see that my knowing was a series of labels I chose to stick on those things that just simply *were*. "Bad" is a label I used in abundance. It was a way to justify laziness and inactivity, and a lack of desire to accept or to overcome my obstacles. Circumstances just *are*. We can label them as good or bad; it is simply a matter of choice supported by our chosen perspective. I always liked the analogy, "the cup is half empty or half full." What is wrong with "the cup has just enough for right now?"

Our mind has the ability to become the author of its own story—one that has not yet happened, and we often choose to make it a tragedy or horror story. It also amazes me the power it has to create fear and inactivity in something that is untrue or has not yet, nor may never happen. Anything other than right now is either gone or not here, and therefore not worthy of worrying about right this second. Projecting delivers tomorrow's challenges today—and if you wait until tomorrow, they may not ever manifest themselves.

I see projecting like a painter. Since our canvas is blank, we can apply our brush in any stroke or pattern using any color we wish. We do not know, ever … **ever**, what the next minute will bring! Outside of right now, the future is a blank canvas we can paint. It develops because of what we think *now*. If the future is not real, not here, not now, and if I choose not to stay here and paint, I therefore, can *choose what to paint!* This epiphany was huge for me. I try to stay present, but occasionally, being human, let go of the line keeping me tethered to the dock. Since the future isn't here, isn't real, isn't now, and has no truth yet, and I can *choose* what to paint and what to think about, why not *choose* a positive picture?

We have all heard about miracles occurring, from Divine intervention to Publishers Clearing House checks appearing at the doorstep. Horses come from behind to beat the odds and win the Kentucky Derby. Unexpected job promotions happen at just the right time. Thus, there is tangible proof that even in the bleakest of circumstances, with absolutely horrible odds, blessings can and do occur, as well as sicknesses cured, and abundance bestowed. So, if the future isn't here, isn't now, isn't real, and isn't true—and we choose what we project, and perception is a choice—why do we choose the horror story?

This truth was life changing for me. If I find myself worrying or projecting, I can detach for a moment and look at my painting. Is it true or not? Is it occurring now? Is there an alternative *painting* I can hang in its place that will better serve me? Is this *knowing* supported by actual evidence or did I conjure it? Can I detach from it and focus on what I am doing now, as what I do and think now determines what happens to me later? Simple questions, simple dialogue.

Now when I paint, it is with a positive, and radiant, and spiritually nurturing brush. If I do create a picture that does not serve me well, I know I can tear it up and paint another. I also realize the most brilliant art I can experience is surrounding me in the present moment. So now I am blessed with regular, fulfilling, and deep sleep. I awaken with the alarm alerting me to a new adventure each day. I enjoy each step going through my morning and my days are richer and more serene.

Someone once told me, that I can start my day over at any point. I liked that advice. Although the days I experience now are similar to the days in my past, I notice a lot less noise and challenges, as well as less exhaustion. My ability to appreciate all things has grown exponentially and continues to increase. I have my moments, as we all do, grabbing my brush and palette in haste. I realize though, I won't fall off the planet and the "bop" on my noggin was just an acorn.

*The first thing I have come to grips with is, that "knowing" and "knowledge" can be two separate things. Knowledge, to me, has no perspective or bias placed upon the subject matter. Knowledge simply is what it is. Knowing however is the personal embracing of the subject matter and often a personal perspective is placed upon it. I have found that in taking a tidbit of knowledge, we can impose an interpretation, or better yet a perception upon it. This allows us to take this tidbit and either adapt or distort the original tidbit of knowledge allowing us to **know** it better. The object or situation simply is what it is, but how we embrace or process it; our "knowing" of it personalizes it—sometimes for our good, sometimes not so good.*

We see many examples of this by how many people can see one thing in a variety of different ways. This essay was an awakening on how I realized I placed labels or my "knowing" upon things, which was usually counterproductive. I manipulated my reality, which did not serve me well. I felt my truths were final and, therefore, I became a victim of my own thoughts and circumstances.

A simple shift in my perception allowed me to better see and process the truth. I can now sleep better, minimize panic, maintain my composure, and accept those people and things that are different from me. I have gained much peace in knowing one simple thing: I really don't know much of anything, and that is okay.

Reflections

Have I held onto or fought for beliefs I found out later were not entirely true?

Was it easy or hard for me to admit this to myself and/or to make amends to others?

What are some beliefs and fears I have today, that if I let go of them, my life would improve?

Do I have trouble admitting when I do not know something?

Do I have trouble admitting when I am wrong?

Do I feel others exhibit this unhealthy behavior?

Would I rather be right or happy?

Look Inside

Stop looking outside of yourself for what you need inside.

This is one of my favorite writings. It shows me how I used to be driven by my ego to search for power, knowledge, connections, and titles to make myself feel better. I sought approval of others and the laurels of accomplishment to fill voids I had been carrying within myself. For the longest time I felt disconnected—from people and what I needed to be whole. I felt my titles and accomplishments dictated my position in the eyes of others in society. I was always looking feverishly to people, places, and objects to elevate me, to fulfill me. After finally getting it, I was able to obtain peace and acceptance. This essay dictates my quest and what I gained on my journey to finding the key to peace and acceptance. If only I would have looked in the right place all along!

Everything was out there. Knowledge: out there. Skill: out there. Peace: out there. Mastery: out there. Others had it; I wanted it. I coveted what the prophets, sages, and experts who succeeded before me had—that elusive secret that could take me to the next level. It was out there for the taking. I believed I had the ability, if I only possessed the key, then the wisdom of the universe would unfurl before me and give me that spiritual "ah-ha!" I would then have what I needed to walk among those I respected.

Instead of seeking material objects, I wanted to be revered for my vast expanse of knowledge and skill. Don't get me wrong, I like toys and enjoy material stuff, but I did not see them as the dangling carrot that motivates me in my life's quest to that which makes me whole. I was after skill, knowledge, and peace of mind. So, rather than try to make the most money upfront, I wanted to hang out and draw upon the connected and those in-the-know.

As a hairstylist by trade, acquiring a skill set was just a simple necessity for me to be able to make a living. Hundreds of hours of elementary and state-mandated training led to many more months of an apprenticeship, followed by classes, and updates adding to my technical repertoire. I also learned that the technical side was honestly a small component of success in my business. It is also beneficial to obtain a polished social demeanor, an ability to be in tune with humanity, well-rounded awareness of community issues, and the ability to connect with your clientele. The skills of maintaining a degree of animation, compassion, charity, and simply a love for your fellow man are also important. If this had been brought to my attention early on, it may have been discouraging as the hairstyling technical skills needed apparently were only part of a curriculum that seemed to be ongoing and never-ending. I had my work cut out for me.

I took classes, read, practiced, and focused incessantly on my goal of knowledge supremacy. I traveled the globe looking for people who had what I needed; buying, training, listening to any drops of wisdom that may make it to my thirsty mind. As I gathered this wisdom, my quest gained momentum. As I acquired more knowledge, more became available. When I met with one master, another with more teachings and truths would materialize in front of me. There was always more truth, and I needed it. I was obsessed; addicted if you will. I would even tell my own students to train with someone, and then instruct them to immediately ask their new mentor who had inspired them. Then I said they should move on to the master's master in their quest for truth. It was a chain, and if you were diligent, you would be able to reach the top of the mountain. I thought that was how it was done.

My obsession, this addiction to obtain knowledge supremacy also transcended my career into other points of interest in my life. I was also a martial artist. The same quest for skill supremacy also led me to crave that which gave me physical power over others. This quest spanned over twenty years. I traveled and trained seeking truth and the skill sets I needed to find the peace, and the ability to dominate any foe, either internal or external. Through diligent research I found a group connected to the bloodline of master martial artist, philosopher, and movie actor Bruce Lee. I hit the jackpot! I was training with Bruce's students and those in the bloodline of his curriculum. I was traveling the country learning skills that surely would take me to the next level of almost superhuman skills and philosophy.

I complimented my martial arts skill with bodybuilding, training with some of the city's best trainers, and over a handful of years, put on many pounds of muscle to go from a lean kick boxer build, to a hulking form. My skills and knowledge accumulation seemed to always pay off. I became a higher ranking student, ran in the school's inner circle, gained my black belt in part of the curriculum, and life was good! I was getting the edge I wanted. With that knowledge came admiration, popularity, and personal gain; or so I thought.

I remember in my hair career I had developed a skill set and a reputation that allowed me to travel, perform onstage, and become widely published. I felt that I was aligned with the knowledge pipeline and was getting to meet and run with some of the industry's top Who's Who. As an instructor, I took my assistants to various seminars and interesting places including New York City, the Mecca of our craft in the United States. We would spend time in the city playing and celebrating, but were there mainly for our next injection of insight, to ascend another rung closer to perfection.

One time, we travelled to New York City to train with a gentleman whom I considered a master. I considered our trainer for the weekend a genius. I liked that he trained with one of our industry legends, who has since passed away, so it was as close as I could get to the creator in this special area of expertise. I did not even participate in the hands-on training this time, as I feared missing a pearl of wisdom that he may dispense. If I were busy in my own work, I may miss the opportunity to obtain another key. I shadowed this man as he sauntered among my students as he was observing them. I clung to him, not intrusively, but always within earshot. I would hear a bit here and there, but they were things I had seen or experienced before. I patiently waited for a new key or a gem.

At the end of the day and a successful seminar completed, my friends retired to a hotel bar nearby. Meanwhile, I asked if I could buy my friend; my mentor, dinner. He agreed, and after a brief reprieve we adjourned to a local café of his choice. It was elegant and understated, and it was one that appeared to be a possible immigrant's family treasure. I was thrilled to have the captive audience of my new mentor and friend. Many often paid for his words and time by the hour and I was getting it free! We started with idle banter. I was polite and pleasant, as well as respectful; my goal was to squeeze out more time and more knowledge from him without coming across gauche. As we recapped the day's class, I eventually got the nerve to ask, "What can I do? I **need** to know what else you can teach me. I want to grow!"

He paused for a moment, and just looked at me. A small grin appeared on his face. He removed his glasses and said in his Italian accent, "You know, Tony, at some time the student has to become the master." The waiter interrupted, allowing the thought to marinate. I realize now, as well as then, I knew I had received "the key." I needed to stop looking outside myself for what I needed inside.

The search for mastery is a circular path not a straight line. The path starts within you, radiates outward, and then returns to you. I feel that we start by seeking knowledge or validation. The journey starts with us. We look to fill ourselves with others' truths. We then seek others to fill this void; to learn from them, to elevate ourselves. Finally we come to realize, at some point, we must return home, to settle into a truth that works for us and our divine connection to ourselves. We start to eliminate the stuff that is no longer useful or true to us. Our own mastery requires us to clean out our closets. What I learned that night is: The student is a master of acquisition, and the master is a student of elimination. The threshold between the two is awareness of where the ego lies.

It begins with a desire for something; a search, a hunger. Then the new found desire becomes a desire for peace; the peace of obtaining the truth. If you listen to the space within you, and seek the connection you already have within you, once nourished, connected, and activated, you yourself will become a valuable resource to finding the mastery you seek by seeking your personal truth. You will listen with humility to the voice within you, with the faith that you are being guided correctly. Your goal will no longer be the best to separate you from the pack, but to be available to serve the pack.

From time to time, the mastery will need to be renovated externally and require outside inspiration, as well as continual conscious contact with that which inspires you spiritually. This may come from classes, congregation or skill updates. We find that what we sought outside ourselves was in us all along. It is our internal spiritual well-being that guides us to what we seek. Often our ego can get in the way of this connection.

I have realized that we don't need to forever seek more skills, more knowledge, and more teachers. At some point, we need to turn our focus inward and re-examine the current truths we hold, and their current value to us. Where do these truths derive from? What is the source of our inspiration?

Once you can explore the path you are on without ego, and its interruptions, you will discover you already have many of the keys you so feverishly seek. Then, mastery will simply mean "I have peace because I have nothing left to prove."

This writing reminds me of a scene out of Bruce Lee's Enter the Dragon. Bruce is discussing a lesson with his young protégé. Bruce points upward and says, "It is like pointing your finger away to the moon." The student fixes his gaze on Bruce's finger and Bruce slaps him on the head and says, "Don't concentrate on the finger or you'll miss all the heavenly glory!"

I was focusing on the "finger", the masters, the knowledge and skills, as opposed to the cultivation of my spirit and my peace within me. Spirit and peace can be found within me, and it often requires some direction, but mastery is often when we whittle away the façade. It is when we can apply the sum of our experiences into a simple wisdom and expression of ourselves and how we have digested our traveled path. When the journey stops searching outward and focuses inward, we will be able to apply what we learn from that journey to true self improvement. It is not about "ego seeking" or "approval seeking" but rather a true application of that which you excel in. When you have nothing left to prove, you receive what you have been searching for all along.

Reflections

Have I been seeking something that has eluded me?

Do I have a skill or expertise in something, yet still seek outside approval?

What separates me from what I want or where I want to be?

Is feeling "important" a priority for me?

Is what I need or want still "out there?"

Why don't I have what I want?

Why haven't I achieved my goals?

Is it possible for me to achieve my goals? What is my plan?

Do I feel I have what I need already within me?

If It Weren't For You, I'd Be Happy

No one can upset us without our permission!

If we seek circumstances to get upset over, or hold others responsible for our serenity, we will remain in a constant state of bombardment with little reprieve. Getting a grip on two major forces that can eliminate or immensely diminish negative states I find myself in are: my **expectations** *of what I felt "shoulda, coulda, or woulda" happened, and* **acceptance** *pertaining to my ability to live life on life's terms.*

This essay is a study of how these two elements greatly affect the arguments, battles, and negative states I find myself in. I realize now it is often my misuse or misinterpretation of situations that would allow me to enter, remain, and perpetuate my state of anger. This also helped me hold on to the belief that others were responsible for how I felt, and that I had no ownership in feeling a certain way.

I spent a majority of my life with the word **welcome** written across my forehead. Not necessarily from the negative sense of being a doormat, (yet that has occurred), but letting people and things in. Not only have I let experiences, love, friends, and family in, but I also let opinions, negativity, and unhealthy emotions such as anger in. I know now that everything I allow in, I must first extend an invitation.

I love people. I love helping them, and I find I am willing to risk certain things to receive a connection with people. I trust, I love, I forgive, I befriend again, and knowing therein lurks the risk of being hurt down the line. I choose this approach opposed to the alternative of seclusion, isolation, cynicism, and narrow-mindedness. I know many who choose the latter pattern to protect them from an inevitable disaster they project upon themselves, and often are able to manifest. The thought being, "If I don't open myself to love, I cannot be hurt." "If I don't trust, I cannot be disappointed." "If I don't interact, I cannot get angry."

Anger was like the best friend I invited to a party, knowing he would get drunk, ruin the party, and break my furniture. Yet, for some reason I continued to invite him. Anger had a knack for bringing along his friends, resentment, regret, disappointment, depression, and animosity. They always found my party and I let them in. They were familiar, and they were never exclusive. They even invited others in who cared to join.

Being angry was often empowering and allowed me to seek others with a similar viewpoint. I could always find someone who hated his job, was mad at the government, had spousal issues, was broke, paid too many taxes, got stuck in traffic, or was mad at the weather. Anger was a magnet. It is easy to find others with similar dispositions, people who choose to rally round a cause rather than diffuse a situation. Anger can create fellowship.

After detoxifying my life, I realize anger and other negative emotions have two strong components: expectation and acceptance. Recently my wife and I had a discussion in which there developed a need for us to merge in acceptance of a situation and diminish our personal expectations (this happens frequently in marriages). We, like many couples, can be on the "same planet, but are from different worlds," which is not necessarily a bad thing at all. For going on nearly two decades of marriage it has worked, and if Yin and Yang can find harmony in complementary opposites, well then so can we. We have our moments as couples do, but have always respected each other's quirks, let's say. Well, at least most of the time.

This exchange I mentioned covered a need for my wife and I to come to an understanding of how individuals express and enjoy themselves, as well as the difficulty in the belief that for us to be happy, we may not be able to find it by requesting that others change their habits for us. We both had our viewpoints, valid to the individual's perspective. The details of the discussion are not important here, but the intriguing thing was this: someone or something outside of me, with no physical control over me created anger within me. I remembered a quote that a friend had shared with me: "I am responsible for my own happiness, so the rest of you are off the hook."

The two components, expectation and acceptance, are two things I look at whenever anger (or any other emotion) infiltrates my being.

First, I have to realize **I** am not angry, but I realize anger is present. **I am not the anger**, but it is in my space. I can detach from it for a moment, put it in front of me, and challenge its necessity and value. Often ego-instigated, the awareness of its presence usually starts immediate deflation of the severity, and then clarity of thought can take its place.

Expectations often emerge and fuel the situation to become more negative. I used to expect so much. I would expect that God would know I wanted to play golf on Sunday and thus make the weather perfect. I would expect my wife to know when to leave me alone, or when I needed company. I expected that my kids would not be so foolish to even think about X, Y, or Z (the stuff we parents think our kids will never do but they do because it's just part of being a kid). I would expect that my employers, or others I would seek approval from, would notice my efforts. I would expect things to happen as fast or as slow as I needed. I would expect physical pain to heal quicker than it did. I would expect people to "get me" or where I am coming from. I would expect people to live their lives on my terms.

I expected a lot. My unrealistic expectations were placed upon people who were **unaware** or **unqualified** to fulfill them. I placed my value and happiness in the opinions and actions of others. I spent so much time looking to the future expecting things, followed by looking over my shoulder with a bunch of "if only's." I would invite anger in to disrupt my mental state; the key word here being the word "invite." What **is** is, and the label I choose to place upon it is my own, and I can control my reaction to it, as the only sufferer of anger's wrath is most frequently the owner.

Expectations are often supported by **acceptance** dilemmas often leveraged by a small, simple word, "why?" "Why would they do that?" "Why can't they see it my way?" "Why does this happen to me?" "Why am I such a loser?" Etc. I spent a lot of time not being able to accept what is, and expected something to change. I would form an opinion and then often choose anger to deal with it. What is always remained; it was at that point I felt physically and mentally negative about it—by choice.

I have come to realize I have two choices: **I can work on it, or I can accept it**. Working on it takes me into a **solution mindset**. Acceptance doesn't mean I have to like something, it just means I have to accept it. It just is, and my opinions and emotions do not change what is, although they do affect how I emotionally and physically adapt to it.

Now, when I am angry, I take a breath and reflect, as well as detach from the situation, and observe the anger as if it were something entering the room I am in. I then look to see if I am creating and experiencing expectations and who is responsible for them. Then I focus on acceptance, realizing **I don't have to like it, I just have to accept it.** Then I have a better chance for a more productive dialogue and positive outcome.

I am still three-quarter redneck, a typical husband, and am filled with character defects. I also love a good debate, but now realize I would rather be happy than right (most of the time). And I know conflict is rarely a healthy answer to differences let alone heated confrontations. This simple prayer, written by Reinhold Niebuhr, has always helped me …

"God grant me the serenity to accept the things I cannot change, Courage to change the things I can; and the wisdom to know the difference!"

---

*Thoughts like "if only you could change 'this' about you, I could be happy" or "If others believed what I believe, we could all get along" create a form of spiritual death. They are caused by the false belief that others hold **your** happiness in their hands. How often have you entered a relationship or situation with unrealistic expectations, and found yourself disappointed? Have you taken a situation of what simply is, and continued to ask "Why?" hoping things would justify themselves to you on your terms? I have learned not to put a question mark where God puts a period. It distracts me from moving forward if I continue to look back and question past occurrences. This practice will make it difficult to change your behavior. The key is to practice.*

Reflections

Am I quick to judge or anger?

Do I think others are responsible for my happiness and how I feel?

Do I believe if "they" changed, things would improve in my life?

Do I have unrealistic expectations of myself and others?

Do I believe others cannot live up to my standards?

Is it difficult for me to accept circumstances that don't go my way?

Do I dwell on things for long periods of time and/or hold grudges?

Has anger hindered my life, job, or relationships?

Do I take ownership of my anger? Expectations? Acceptance?

Remember To Love The One You're With

Often we withhold love from those who love us the most, and forgiveness from those who forgive us the most!

This essay proved to be an eye opener for me. It is a story of prioritization and is something I invite everyone to really, deeply reflect upon. The underlying theme is relatively simple. It is kind of a Golden Rule, "do unto others" thing, but to also notice where and when we go left-of-center emotionally. I reflect here on how I interact with my family, loved ones, and even my friends taking them for granted.

What often occurs behind closed doors in our own homes is often where a lot of disruption, disconnection, or resentments can occur. The place where we can feel most connected, loved, and at ease, as well as safe, is where we let our proverbial hair down and expose our beloved to those traits in us that are our least becoming. I think we expect our loved ones to forgive and accept us no matter how we treat them. We expect an abyss of unconditional forgiveness with no repercussions or adjustments in our relationship and home environment. Ironically, aren't these the people to whom we should bestow our best behaviors? Our spouses, parents, and children often receive the brunt of our dark sides. Sadly in some cases, this leads to alienation, divorce, and violence.

Our families deserve our best, and home should be a place where we can spiritually and emotionally recharge, so we are energized when we are required to share of ourselves in society.

I have always been proud of my ability to be in the right place at the right time when it comes to helping others. My career as a hairstylist placed me in a position to where I could not only make a living by making people look and feel good, but also allowed me the capability to use my position to help more than just my clients. Over time, my career allowed me a small niche on a local television station as an "expert" on hair and fashion. That eventually evolved into including segments on wellness, health, and various topics on lifestyle upgrades.

Over six years, my segment took me to a variety of places, events, and businesses. I really enjoyed being able to share positive stories and give visibility to numerous people and causes on top of the beauty pieces I did. I think people have come to realize that I am a sucker for a proverbial damsel in distress, and love using my abilities to help those needing or deserving help. I have been pleasantly surprised to see the genuine heart people have, especially the media, when they are often unfairly scrutinized for a presumed lack of compassion. Many times have I seen friends I have come to know in the media, and other so-called "privileged positions," rise to the call to help the underdog and their fellow man. It really makes my heart smile.

If I could ever have a super power it would be the ability to heal. I can't stand to see struggle, strife, sadness, or pain in others. At any given moment, I will help little old ladies, kiss babies, and shovel snow for a neighbor needing assistance. I have probably done more free services in my career than many have charged for, and I am on a perpetual quest to locate humanitarian opportunities to be a part of. Yes, they make me feel good, but my motive is to help others and to set an example of how we should live, even if no one is there to see it. I don't broadcast it, I just do it.

The morning in question started much like any other as the family awoke to a new week. I am in charge of getting our two beautiful children rallied from rest in the morn, and my wife flies solo in a personal fury of hair and makeup routines. I love being the first thing our kids see in the morning and the last at night. I stir the kids, hop in the shower, brew the coffee, and relax with the news for a few minutes before venturing upstairs to choose the days' attire. I get the kids rolling as my wife will proceed to our business early to handle the things I don't much care to do, and for that I am thankful.

I found I was coaxing and coaching the kids with short barks, bellers, and bitches, and for no apparent reason. Maybe my expectations were not being met by a ten-year-old and a five-year-old on forty-four-year-olds terms. They could not move fast enough or with enough skill, nor perform on or at my pace. When my wife greeted me with a cheerful "Good morning", I responded with a monosyllabic grunt. Three of the people most deserving of my love, respect, and attention, as well as my duty to help them feel peace and serenity at home, are quite often the last to receive it.

When I dropped off the kids at their respective daycare facilities, I missed them, kissed them, and began the internal countdown to when I would see them again that evening. I also immediately reflected on how I had acted that morning and felt remorseful. I have become aware of this character defect in me, and realize awareness is the first step to correcting it, but I still find myself acting this way at times. It surprises me as I have spoken with others about the harm we subject our beloved to through our withdrawal, verbal abuse, and disconnection to their needs, and how prevalent it is. It is like we expect them to have superhuman power shields to protect them from our emotional Kryptonite.

Our spouses, kids, and parents are most deserving of our love, forgiveness, understanding, and support—yet they are often the ones who get the "B-grade" leftovers of us. It is not to say that things are always unsettled or stormy, but if I witnessed someone act in this way to someone they loved, I know I would think "that guy is a horse's ass!" I realize that sometimes I can be that guy, and I am not proud of it.

I realize I will drive across town to help a stranger, but might not get off the couch to get my wife a beverage, in spite of all she does for me. I might not stop reading email or surfing the web to listen to my daughter read to me, or share an important happening in her day; that I might not dignify a goofy peek-a-boo trick my son performs with a smile because I am too busy. Now to some, these behaviors may seem trivial and insignificant (which to me they aren't), but these behaviors eventually gain interest and momentum. Think of these done repeatedly in your home, to your loved ones daily, over years even, and observe where these behaviors can evolve into more difficult obstacles to erode your relationships. They can grow like weeds in a garden.

At least I am aware of my behavior, which prevents these activities from going unnoticed; and I can hold myself accountable. I try to put myself in the shoes of the person receiving my ill will. For example, if someone says "Good morning", and I offer no response or utter a grumbled reply or a glare, I observe from their perspective how I would feel, then I make amends as soon as I am able. I don't always bat a thousand, but now I see the wrong in it, and am trying. I also look at it from the perspective of how I would feel if someone treated my family and friends with the same rude indifference that I have spewed before.

I notice how much better I feel when I treat those around me, especially my loved ones, better and in the way they deserve. I receive love, kindness, and respect—a return on my investment immediately in most cases that is well worth the effort.

It is good training to serve others and be an asset to your community. Giving, receiving, and witnessing kindness is truly good for the soul. The bottom line, though, is to help others where you can, live by example, and work on your spiritual credit rating. And never ever forget to love the ones you're with!

---

*I used to compare myself to others to make myself feel better. For example, "I can't be **that** bad", or "I am not a big yeller", or "I don't spank or beat my kids", or "I have never laid a hand on a woman." These were justifications and rationalizations I used to distract me from my own selfish behaviors. Rather than cultivate a better life and better relationships, I lived by doing just enough to get by or to simply walk the line, when often the line was not paying off at all—for me or others. I tried to avoid conflict, but to no avail. I denied those around me my best self. I would often be drained by trying to figure out how to save the world outside my home while forsaking the best place to practice what I sought to be able to do for the masses. I was there **with** my family, but not always there **for** my family.*

I now strive to serve and love those closest to me first; then I expand my circle of influence and service from there. This is and has been a work in progress; a lot of personal retraining that takes time. The payoffs in this are monumental and transcend their boundaries; their benefits appear in all facets of our lives if we can practice this. On the other hand, not paying attention to the needs of those around me, and treating them with the dignity they deserve, puts me at risk of losing them and all I hold dear. Then the only one who will be left to hear me complain is me.

Reflections

Do I treat those closest to me with less than they deserve?

If I saw someone else treat my family the way I do, how would I react?

When I become aware I have acted inappropriately to my loved ones, do I try to make amends?

Do I value how I look more to people outside my home than in?

Do I usually consider those in my home to be "in the way" or a blessing?

How can I improve my interactions with those closest to me?

Do I distance myself from those who desire my presence?

Do I do enough in my surroundings or could I contribute more? If so, in what way(s)?

Do I set a good example or do I have room for improvement? How?

The Beacon

My faith is like an umbrella; it doesn't remove me from the storm, but I get less wet while patiently awaiting the rainbow.

This essay may evoke critique and controversy, but I sincerely hope not, as my intent is not to proselytize, but rather discuss a personal experience and how certain tools and beliefs have helped me navigate through my emotional obstacles. Since it is an elementary observation of my connection with a "Divine" place, I implore you to not look at these beliefs as all-inclusive, finite, or where my opinions eternally remain. It is a snapshot in time about how reliance on something or someone greater than oneself can soothe a troubled soul. I also ask that if you find any offense or differences, please forgive me as my request to you is to simply appreciate the story of a man who was used to going it alone, and then started to explore how incorporating certain principles could have a tangible and emotional benefit.

My morning started with a two-hour drive to celebrate the memory of a fallen friend. We met in a program of recovery and spent a brief but focused amount of time together. He reached out to me occasionally, I answered when I could. He had angst and demons that had a strong hold on him. Eventually and most untimely, he was taken from this earth at the age of thirty-two.

I stood and watched as those who loved him mourned, young and old trying to make sense of the senseless. Tears, hugs, and the deep dark toll of a church bell celebrated his soul's freedom from human pain. The sun warmed me as the bells serenaded my slow plodding footsteps, which took me past the family and friends who were engaged in soft banter contemplating the void in their lives. I turned with a final glance upward, said thank you to my friend for his "message" and then ventured back to my car.

Upon arriving home, I was greeted with the casual goings on of children on a summer day eating PB&Js. They offered passive dialogue exchanges that allowed me the peace to deal with the morning's events. Stoic is all I can say to describe my demeanor.

I changed out of my black suit into casual attire: a peace sign T-shirt, jeans, and boat shoes. I was gearing up to visit a dear friend at the hospital who underwent surgery that morning. She is a joy to be in the presence of; a beautiful woman with a warm personality. Knowing her is one of the best gifts I have ever received. Several years ago she was diagnosed with a progressive disease which has changed her life through a series of obstacles not only physical, but financial, marital, and beyond. Adding a recent diagnosis of diabetes, and the surgery that placed her in a hospital bed this day, I am pained for her and pray for a miracle of Biblical, even epic, proportions. In spite of these challenges though, she remains a song. The music of her spirit is intoxicating.

It was hard seeing her lying on her side, woozy and wired to the medical equipment. In the company of her mother, she lay fetal with her stuffed animal, finding comfort at forty from that which children crave, but it was alright and the animal looked as much at peace as she did. I entered after a gentle knock, and presented her with a beautiful bouquet of flowers. She lit up like a Christmas tree, her smile filling the room and her spirit coming to life. After hearing of my morning, even in the fog of narcotics, she still mustered words of hope, strength, and peace to me for the friend I had lost. She was actually the one comforting me. She is like that. She puts others first.

Even though I wrestle with how or why things happen, I know I have to stay connected and focused. Where anger, bitterness, sorrow, despair, denial, and defiance used to infiltrate my soul, I now realize there are tools, principles, insights, practices, and personal assessments I can do to simply make sense of things. I can do my part to elevate my spirit upward, which in turn can leverage my perception and ability to find joy in situations as opposed to sorrow or helplessness.

When I was going through a rough time battling my own demons, I was required to attend a series of lectures to enlighten me on how to improve my quality of life. I loved Thursdays, as the topic of Thursdays was spirituality. Being a relatively positive guy, and having been a motivational speaker of sorts, I always felt "pretty good." As

I reflect now, however, I was living on the lesser side of evil, rather than the greater side of good. What I mean is I was doing enough of the "good guy" stuff to get by, gaining external favor and not getting into too much trouble. I was working at not being "too bad" as opposed to trying to cultivate peace within myself or focusing in the now. I was doing just enough to get by, to not feel or be considered bad, walking that line, as opposed to seeking ways to improve my life and my outlook upon it. I didn't focus on making my life better; I just avoided getting into trouble; like I was a middle-aged teenager.

Thursday's lectures were given by another gem of a man, a kind soul, a warm heart, and one who has walked in the shoes of the audience he spoke in front of. He was a Director of Pastoral Care of a local hospital, but his words made me picture him more of a life preserver in my storm. I had fallen victim to addictions, self-inflicted stress, self-loathing, and felt forsaken by God. Something told me to listen to him and listen well. This journey had begun and I was no longer driving.

The lecture started by our spiritual director scribing in dry erase marker on the whiteboard: Faith, Religion, and Spirituality. I used to think they were the same thing, but my mentor proved me wrong. I will elaborate on what I have learned and what helps me daily, to leverage myself against succumbing to the ego and self-inflicted angst.

My definition of faith is best expressed in an abbreviated quote I will loosely paraphrase from the Bible: "Blessed are those who believe without seeing." I used to think faith solely meant a practice or a denomination, like "What faith are you?" Now, rather than exclusively a religious denomination, I also see faith as a state I can find myself in. Faith helps me deal with the unexplainable, unforeseeable, and intangible. Like projection, it is a picture in which my choices can create the content of my current well-being. I can choose to practice faith, to believe things are as they should be, they are of a Divine nature, and all is for my greater good. Faith is a positive practice of staying connected to my spirituality and allowing things to happen. This couples with the realization that they will not necessarily happen on my terms.

I find it hard to have faith and be cynical at the same time. For me, it is either "door number one" which contains faith and positive energy and Divine direction, or "door number two" which contains sorrow, sadness, self-victimization, and the feeling of impending doom. Both are choices; choose wisely.

Religion, to me, is a series of practices, rituals, fellowships, dogmas, and texts used to enhance one's connection to a belief system and/or deity. Religion is a way to show belonging and practice. For some people it dictates a path to follow, a method to achieving one's personal connection to that which they believe in. The ultimate underlying theme of most religions lend themselves to: a love for their fellow man and all creatures, observance of a creative power, source, essence or deity, what happens to one after death, parameters of acceptable behavior, as well as how and where to practice and profess their beliefs.

Both faith and religion can be complementary and exclusive; one can exist without the presence of the other. They are tools to achieve peace and fellowship as well as personal connection to a divine space.

Spirituality was explained to me as a "connection to yourself, your fellow man, and a Higher Power of your understanding." I liked learning that I could be or become spiritual without having to subscribe to anything just yet. Spirituality allowed me to find peace with certain personal standards. It is a quest of making sense of my connection to all things Divine. I enjoy seeing things without judgment. I gain peace through improved understanding, and I seek to find it in me and around me. My path is mine, yours is yours. We can listen, share, grow, and enjoy serenity in the process of seeking mutual understanding. My spirituality is what tells me if my religion is right for me. It gives me faith and gets me through. I have a new understanding and my path is much more vivid and seems right for me.

These three components saved me and sustain me during the times in my life like the ones I mentioned earlier in this essay. My understanding gives me calm in the storm and the tools to proceed when it is tough to move forward.

I invite you to seek your own definitions of the "big three." Discover how they fit into your life. Utilize the principles of faith, religion, and spirituality so they can become your beacon during the storms.

I find peace in things I cannot immediately explain or understand. My faith, religion, and spirituality calm me and give me a feeling that there is a harbor in the storm. I find meaning in the meaningless and consolation in an often-troubled world. My path gives me patience and peace while I wait for questions to be answered and my paths revealed. Again, this is not to impose my beliefs on you, or to imply that any one way is for everyone. I simply ask you to explore ways that expose you to true life meaning as you proceed toward your personal connection with that which enriches your life.

Reflections

What beliefs, rituals, or practices are there for me when I need them?

Do I desire a greater connection with "something greater?"

What energizes me spiritually?

Does the thought of a spiritual or divine force intimidate me?

Do I often feel alone in times of need, feeling there is no higher power or "something greater?"

How do I stay connected spiritually with my beliefs?

Can I find comfort, answers, and connection when I need them?

Reflect on your personal interpretations of faith, religion, and spirituality.

She Burnt The Eggs

My greatest fear is not my inability to practice what I preach; but my inability to become aware when I am not doing so.

Here I take a simple mundane event that had no connection or relevance to me whatsoever, and show how I captured it, owned it, and rearranged it to where I found myself in a disruptive state. It lingered and also subsequently caused a skewed perception in my dealings with other people. In writing this I was having fun, perhaps as a defense mechanism and maybe out of the juvenile actions that came from what I thought was a somewhat stable, educated, middle-aged man. This incident helps me see how downright silly we can behave at times. Humorous to me now, at the time of its occurrence, it was sadly rather real to me.

  Somehow, somewhere, I must have become important enough to put me in the crosshairs of a conspiracy. There was a strong plot and there was intelligence behind it; the forces were masters of stealth, as I never truly faced off with my adversaries. Like poison darts from natives hiding in the jungle in an old Tarzan movie, I felt the sting and knew they were close by. I couldn't relax and always had to be on my toes. Something or someone was out to get me; to disrupt my life and happiness. I eventually became adept at identifying these forces. I not only became aware, I gained a super-heightened sensitivity. When something would occur, I could instantaneously pin the incident on my adversaries and quickly call them out. No matter how good I got at identifying them, another agent or booby trap was waiting. Why me? Why the conspiracy? All I wanted was peace, yet they were out to do me in.

One evening I decided to forgo some obligations to spend quality time with my family. We were going to entertain friends the next evening, so I decided a lap around the yard with a mower was in order. My wife weeded and our kids did what kids do. We have a small, but peaceful yard with many trees and plants. The center of my yard belongs to my kids' trampoline and swing set. I have come to enjoy my patio, and my landscaping has matured to provide an atmosphere of isolation from the neighbors; and the trees flanking my property flourish and there is never a loss for birdsongs. It is my own little nirvana. We finished the yard work and retired to the house at dusk.

Dinner, TV, some magazine thumbing, phone calls, and random kitchen chores for my wife closed out our evening. The kids were silent in a good way, and I was on the computer doing random Internet surfing. My office is positioned off the living room and is separated by two French doors from the patio I love. I can close or open the doors, inviting family and nature in, or shut them out depending on my mood or what is on my agenda.

Since the TV was entertaining my wife, the door leading to the house was closed, as were the doors to the patio. The summer bugs were attracted to my office lights and computer monitor so I kept the doors closed this summer evening. I was waiting for the sun to go down as I have found a love for retiring to the patio at night to practice Qigong in front of the blue glow of my bug zapper. The "entomological executions" are drowned out by mood music on my MP3 player, and my motions are mirrored by shadows dancing on the house's façade. I look forward to this mental detox ritual as the day's duties can often be draining, and I will sleep like a baby if left alone and in solitude.

As the sun dropped, I sat in the office in anticipation of my relaxation and some me time. Blessed with a space of peace just outside my door, where no one can get me, I am a lucky man. The sun made its descent and I turned off the computer, grabbed my music player, and opened my office door to the living room. "Dad is going outside, please give him privacy" was the message I delivered. After a noticeable disinterest in my departure, I heard a couple loud "pops" come from the kitchen. No one was in the kitchen, so the sound anomalies needed investigation. The realization came to me as I said to my wife, "You were cooking hard-boiled eggs earlier. Did you ever take them off the stove?" Her look of horror and surprise gave me the answer I needed.

We scurried off to examine the carnage. She exclaimed surprise at the fact that eggs could turn that color in their shells when burnt. I took it upon myself to remind her of the principles of evaporation. She took the pan of scorched eggs and decided that running cold water from the faucet would stop the popcorn-like reaction. The steam that geysered up from the pan, although dangerous and a shock to my wife, was nothing compared to the smell that wafted and enveloped the first floor of the house. Somewhere between a fart and burning hot garbage is what I remember labeling it. As my wife stood there, with her burned eggs and the possibility of her "locally-famous" deviled eggs destroyed, I realized she was one of them. They had finally infiltrated my home.

I proceeded to blame her for messing up my atmosphere. I forced a few gagging noises resulting from the smell. I was appalled at how she could cause this and have it affect me. My night was in shambles. I retreated to my office in a huff and burned some incense to mask the noxious odor. I knew it would remain. How could she cause this unsettling disaster to undermine my serenity and solitude? I retreated to the patio to find at least a shred of the peace that had been rudely taken from me. Why me? Why is everyone trying to get me?"

As I began my attempt to center and calm myself, my daughter emerged from the office door to ask if we could hang out together later. My disgust came with a realization that she was one of them too! I could not relax if people would not let me. I blamed her for my disconnection from my peaceful meditation and told her to leave me at once.

I once again centered and attempted my routine, but it was difficult as I was now so disrupted and I knew they would get me again. I was the target of their irritating folly. I went through the motions, yet my mind waited for the next interruption, and my expectations were met when my daughter emerged once again with our Shih Tzu. I removed my ear buds and bellowed, "What now?!" She stammered that the dog had to pee in an unsettled tone, but in my confrontation, I must've scared the pee back into the dog as it bolted back inside, followed by my daughter slamming the door behind her. My routine remained unscathed from there and I finally got settled down. I made amends to the family and the night proceeded, from my perception, as if all was smooth sailing. My wife was fine, the dog peed, and my daughter and I bonded.

The next morning, my kids reminded me of their roles as being one of them as they made some simple kid messes, and I blamed them for our horrible living conditions and that I never can have a clean house with all the "pigs" trying to get me. I did my share of spite cleaning, as they did theirs, and I focused on the kitchen as our guests were to arrive that night and I wanted to tidy up the house. As I loaded the dishwasher, I came across the pan that was the incineration chamber for the eggs. The bottom of the pan was scorched black with the random outlines of the eggs unfortunate enough to be closest to the flame. I scanned the bottom of the pan for a few moments. This time there was no blame, no animosity, no judgment; I just looked.

The pan signified many things. It was a target of my egocentric rants and blame. It was a symbol I held that was not unlike the many people, places, and things I blamed for other lapses in my composure. Things like broken shoestrings, slow people crossing the street, bird poop on the windshield, forgotten bills, telemarketers, price hikes, my kids interrupting me, clothes not fitting, being low on gas, errands, grass growing, and the multitude of things I cannot control. It is simply the **life** that is happening around me daily that I choose to perceive is seeking me out to disrupt or destroy me. Yes me, the one so important that the cosmos aligned to poke at until I go insane.

My wife didn't burn the eggs. The heat that was meant to cook our food eventually allowed the water to escape into the atmosphere creating an unstable condition not conducive to palatable egg doneness. She simply got distracted, as would I, after reclining in recovery from an afternoon of tedious yard work. There was no conspiracy, only my desire to blame and to not take accountability of my perception of a random, insignificant occurrence that had no major negative repercussions or duration. My perception and childish outlook endured far longer than the incident. I was the only one who created and owned the physical disruption from a simple harmless event. I am thankful for this epiphany and hope it sticks. I am glad to not be that important, and realize there is no conspiracy. Aside from the eggs, the only thing that got burned that night was me.

* Note – While this project was in edit, I too burnt the eggs. My wife enjoys reminding me.

Has something like this ever happened to you? As I try to evolve, I attempt to be aware when I start to own more than I can truly lay claim to. I see now, when simple occurrences are shifted into perceived personal attacks, therefore enabling a victim mindset and an unquenchable desire for retribution and blame. I see in some cases how we can elevate the severity of the situation simply by our interpretation using proclamations such as "once again", or "as always." These statements allow us to perceive some randomly occurring situation to be a repetitious, ongoing onslaught focused on disarming us and that we are a victim.

It is hard to admit we are being irrational and overly sensitive, and are seeking a scapegoat, so we try to pin the situation on someone and add negative harm-inducing motives behind it. I see how often I would take simple daily normal life circumstances and see them as attacks and Lord help whoever was the one who left the cereal box open as "It was on!" I can't say that I am perfect and have totally eliminated these stupid flare-ups, but at least I realize that I am not the target of a global conspiracy, and maybe at times I should just switch to decaf.

Reflections

Do I identify with the story in any way?

Do I think other people are out to get me, or at least get to me?

Do I redirect neutral occurrences as attacks upon me?

Do I accuse others of intentionally doing things that are often coincidental or accidents?

Can I see where taking a moment to seek another perspective could reduce some conflicts in my life?

Does my desire to own the event and see myself as the victim cause me pain or emotional discomfort?

I Choose To Not Participate

What you focus on is what you will see.

The choice to participate in certain discussions or disputes is a profound one that can deeply affect how your day goes. After reading this essay, I realized my shift was starting to take root in my core. My thoughts have become more positive with less effort. My practices are starting to take hold. I have come to understand where the threshold between what I can control, and what I cannot control is.

I see how we can often seek comfort from others who help remind us of our misery when we are feeling low, as opposed to searching for a hand to lift our spirits. I have observed that sometimes, as a form of entertainment, people look to the media to see how bad things are to support their own personal view of something. This seems to give them satisfaction in their ill feelings as well as a desire for retribution they can impose upon "those deserving" while inviting others to participate.

I am fortunate to live in a nice area of a nice city in the Midwest. I enjoy suburbs, strip malls, parks, and pleasant surroundings which make it a nice place to raise a family. The area I live in is located near a cluster of inviting small communities that look like Norman Rockwell had a hand in their development. We are also located right next to our local university that emanates a certain youthful energy year-round. You can almost feel the bass drums of the marching band playing our fight song in the fall.

I have always liked the fact that our city is relatively easy to navigate. We have major thoroughfares that bisect the city, while others run around the circumference. You can easily get to one end of our city to the other in about twenty minutes with forgiving traffic. It is a city of about 1.2 million inhabitants where we all enjoy many of the communities' amenities and not just those closest to us.

I would say with much pride, that our city's officials do make it a priority to focus on the aesthetic as well as functional operations of our city. We do have our problem areas, as all cities do, but for the most part, if it is not currently being tended to, it is on the list. From the inner-city redevelopment, giving common area surfaces a facelift, and general concern for the future, I can say I'm relatively pleased overall with where my tax dollars go and I do indeed see progress, both short and long-term. Others may disagree, but personally, I am content.

I have reached a level of comfort driving in a larger city, having grown up in a small town. Still at times, our local interstates and byways become a proving ground for people's racing prowess and patience. They can also be a necessary daily hurdle to either go to work, or achieve a completed chore list. Unlike very large cities, (we are around the seventeenth largest), we can also use the streets in our suburbs, although limited by slower speed limits and traffic lights. Life can go on without entering the highways' hustle and bustle.

As with bicycles and beach balls, we have gotten used to the familiar and prolific appearance of orange barrels in our streets and thoroughfares as sign of summer. In the past twenty years of living in the city, I can say they have not let me down any more than the arrival of the seasonal fireflies. (For those unaware, orange barrels are the manmade barriers used around road construction and repair by the Department of Transportation to show that our tax dollars are at work and where we can safely travel.) After a few months of inconvenience, be assured that we will be traveling on velvety smooth roads once again.

This summer did not disappoint. The roadway scheduled for repair happened to be a main byway that conveniently ran through the city and connected many of its suburbs. This road is also a main artery taking people into and out of the city's heart. I probably do not need to mention that there was public unrest and dissent, and much speculation focused on when this project should best be completed, at whose cost, and for how much money. These discussions were partnered with much projection on how much "chaos and maddening inconvenience" we could expect. Traffic Armageddon was coming, and only six blocks from my house! I was waiting for the torches and pitchforks to come out. Much time had been dedicated to the project in the local media, most of it focused on the impending inconveniences. I have not heard much about the benefits we will receive once the construction project is finished.

While surfing my homepage on a popular social networking site, I saw that a couple friends who are anchors for a local television network had posted a few threads. The thread that caught my attention prompted people to explain their views on the recently initiated road project. The comments projected upcoming inconveniences: how "others" were going to drive, how drives to work would be extended by at least a few minutes, and how crazy and chaotic life was going to be. I had since forgotten about the project in my neighborhood, but thought, "Should I be worried, stock up on canned goods, hoard gasoline, and perhaps pull all my money out of the bank?" After reading a few, okay about a dozen, of the posts, I posted a comment: "God forbid we have to get up a few minutes early or use MapQuest. Take it easy and enjoy the ride!" My post lay unanswered for about thirty minutes, when a person I do not know chimed in: "Tony, spoken like someone who is unaffected by the project."

Well, the redneck ego in me could not allow it to go, even though I was shopping at our local lawn and garden store with my kids when I read the message. God bless technology, as I was able to respond promptly on my iPhone: "Actually I live a few blocks away and I am directly affected. I just realize I have to accept it and be patient is all." Someone else I did not know chimed in: "Guess you told them, Tony!" Telling them was not my intent as much as establishing where I stood in regard to the posts exclaiming anger and despair. I finalized my contribution to the thread with: "I just realize that no one can piss me off without my permission. Although I completely understand the frustration, I just choose to not participate." The posts resumed with more pitiful projections, laments, and general whining; eventually I lost interest.

This exchange, this focus on negativity helped me realize that venting without searching for a solution or attempt to dissolve the situation is a futile waste of energy. Websites, publications, and rallies can be useful tools to enlighten and recruit energy from people with a goal to dissipate the disruption. They are also great ways to solve a crisis or to add more people to the movement. At times, if done in a positive light, momentum can be gained. I do lament though, for those people who voyeuristically or gratuitously sit on the sidelines and fan the fire with anger and terse words, in hopes someone else will solve their personal issues. I see an epidemic of people's desire to watch and bitch. I realize if I want to become sadder, angrier, or more depressed, or more appalled, I have an army of individuals to stand with me, and enough resources that could fill the shelves at the Library of Congress. Since I can only truly focus and give positive attention to a limited number of things, why would I consciously choose to be scared, appalled, or angered by choice? Informed is one thing, but often considered by many as not as fun!

I now find solace, not through oblivious disconnection, but through practicing awareness of, "Am I part of the problem or part of the solution" as my position of involvement. I remember being told: "Don't bitch about anything you do not wish to take over!" I try to stay aware and informed, but choose not to fan my own flames. I have enough true and tangible circumstances that affect me and my loved ones that require my time and attention. I do get involved in the community, where my efforts are appreciated and contribute to the greater good. I realize there are many armchair politicians holding "caucuses", as well as media, news, and print all beckoning for my attention. There is a huge, open-invite, pity party sending me frequent invitations. As I have said before, "Although I completely understand, I simply choose to not participate."

---

*I still remember this day and the few lines of text that prompted the writing. I simply had enough griping, not just there but everywhere. I no longer will relinquish my ability to seek the good in things, by others wishing to share loudly how **bad** things are, and how **bad** they are going to be. I don't have to watch it, read about it, or take a big mouthful of the toxic soup that is presented to me. I now find it foolish to seek out and tune into others complaining, let alone to participate. If I cannot either lend support, experience, hope, or love, I would rather save my energies until I can positively contribute.*

Reflections

Do I enjoy gossip and hearing about other people's negative situations?

Do I share these stories with others and the sooner the better?

Do I find gossip-based or human suffering shows (like court room dramas, trauma, or divorce) entertaining?

Do I often refer to or identify with these programs in my life?

Do the programs I watch entertain, energize, or drain me? Why?

Could I abstain in part or totally from negative conversations or participating in nonproductive environments?

What are the challenges to eliminating these things from my life? Would my life improve?

The Rest Is Just Gravy

Happiness in our life can be improved by our comprehending the definitions of *wants* and *needs*.

"The rest is just gravy" is an expression I heard growing up in a small town. It simply means icing on the cake, or the added bonus of something. Many people, as they age and mature, go through a re-prioritization of what is important in their lives. I experienced this shift when facing my personal "behavioral health" issues. In this essay, I wonder why we seem to focus on some things in our lives with such fervor and with such purpose—and then, in an instant, we no longer desire or value them? Why does that shift occur?

What I have learned is that typically after a shift—deciding that having, doing, or achieving less is at times more desirable if placed in the proper context—people experience a greater sense of peace, as well as a feeling of being surrounded by abundance.

It was after high school and I found myself with the typical parental pressure to go to college. I was fortunate in the fact that high school came easy for me, and without even trying I was able to graduate at the bottom of the top of my class. I was listed in the graduation flyer as having graduated "with distinction" which was good enough for me. My name was in print, diploma in hand, and I had a newfound freedom to explore adulthood on my terms, and to become a success.

After a summer of debauchery, I entered Ohio State University that fall. My grades allowed it, I was expected to, and I wanted to please my family. I figured that through osmosis I would eventually get into it and assimilate, learning how to study and focus, as high school did not prepare me. My wits and whatever intellect I had, allowed me to cross that finish line with little effort. I had enough charisma to usually get what and where I needed, and figured college would be no different. I signed up for Business Management as my major, but I applied myself exclusively to the curriculum of bars, girls, and martial arts training. I would highlight my week occasionally with a class or two.

After three quarters and a soaring 1.9 GPA, I retreated in shame to my hometown to resume the curriculum I started in college. I rationalized that I could easily study bars, girls, and martial arts without costing my folks the tuition the college required, and be close to my old friends. I knew I would eventually be successful, just on my terms. I defended my behavior proclaiming I proved I could make the grades if I was into something, I just wasn't into college. I tried months later to attend a Technical College, added pool hustling to my studies, lasted seven weeks, and quit. The real world 2. Tony 0.

I retreated again to my hometown and found myself surrounded by like-minded people and success was not really a focus for them at the time. I longed for it, but did not work for it, as I had a picture of what success was, but felt I was not ready. Movies of that time period starred the Brat Pack, like St. Elmo's Fire, and the Breakfast Club which validated my angst and gave me role models to emulate. I felt that being deep and brooding, lamenting change and that life was passing me by was my role in this world. Boy it was rough being twenty-one in America in the eighties!

My father was a self-made man at that point, and was a successful businessman, author, and motivational business speaker. He was a man on the go, I rarely saw him, (my parents divorced when I was five), and he traveled the world and inspired others. He had the fancy cars, the businesses, and leadership to get what and where he wanted. He was locally as well as nationally known, but not so much in my upbringing. I harbor no animosity as I thought that was simply how you got successful. "You have to have your priorities in check," he would tell me. He had the position and the possessions, and it appeared his philosophy was paying off. He worked very hard for his success.

After my second strike at schooling, my father called and asked to pick me up for the day. I lived with my mother and step-father and younger sister about an hour away from my father. It was in the middle of the week, which was atypical as he usually had obligations that only allowed him to be with us kids on random weekends when he was in town. He used to proudly state that for a two-year stretch, he worked every day for seven days straight, only getting Christmas and Easter weekends off, other than that he was booked every day. What surprised me about the impromptu visit is we usually had to plan our visits in advance due to his schedule. However, I concurred and he picked me up. He mentioned he had a business friend he wanted to introduce me to. My dad's friends were always really cool, "good ole' boys", successful, or combination of all the above. I can't think of any I really did not like or whose company I did not enjoy.

We arrived after a short drive and light conversation and pulled into his friend's up-and-coming company in which my father had become a consultant and industry liaison. In the parking lot there were luxury cars, and tanned, beautiful people represented the staff. High energy and purpose coursed through the halls. It was a family business and they all were on board making things happen. All were confident, well-dressed, and appeared busy. They scurried about, spouted words about things like "purchase orders" and "shipping", spoke of dollar amounts in the thousands, hovered over copy machines, and had those motivating plaques with catchy sayings posted all over the place. I was impressed with the owner as he walked fast with a furrowed brow and always seemed to be intensely contemplating something "businessy". This was success and I wanted in!

My visit that day with my dad was less of a visit and more of an abduction to save me from my small town which was becoming a kind of Venus fly trap devouring me slowly. I started working there by labeling bottles in the warehouse and eventually over time, became an assistant to the marketing director. Not bad for my early twenties! During our downtime we enjoyed champagne, beautiful girls, fine cars, cruises, and cash. It was great on the outside, but on the inside I knew there were still levels of success to be achieved.

After hitting the proverbial glass ceiling in the family business, my father approached me about pursuing my initial goal of coming on board into his company, and training in cosmetology. I thought all I would have to do is get the required state mandated training, work through the ranks, and enjoy the fruits of a family business.

I completed the curriculum at the top of my class, and realized I had an intuitive skill set. After some short lived crucifixion that the child of any executive may get entering into the family business, the cries of nepotism subsided giving way to an embrace by my peers. Early on, I had the condo, sports car, and made decent money. I traveled and got my share of recognition subsidized by my family, as well as the power of the company and its local visibility. I had the hot dates and VIP passes to clubs, and was perceptively happy at the time enjoying this climb to success. Although materially happy, I still felt there must be more.

Eventually I married a beautiful young woman who I worked with, which supported common interests, and she could travel with me on business, sharing the company tab all the while bettering her career at the seminars we attended. After a few modest dwellings, we moved into our current home in a coveted suburb of the city where nice homes, parks, lush landscaping, and the exclusive mindset prevail. Material rewards appeared, as did our dream of two beautiful children, which are our gifts from heaven. This was success! Or was it?

Over time I realized I longed for something that still eluded me. Was it leadership, the ability to be a decision-maker, or a public figure I longed for? I didn't know, but I was blessed in the toy department, I had two beautiful kids, the beautiful wife; check, check, and check, so why was I feeling this void? My relationship with my father eventually soured over time, and I realized our values and personalities were fundamentally different. As of this writing, we are indefinitely estranged and no longer work together.

After my exit from my father's business I decide to do it my way and opened my own company. I was very pleased that many years of creating friendships and networking in the community paid off. Many people, both notable and in the media, came to my aid. I thought, "Now this must be success!" I had a company, the who's who of our city was all lending their support, and now more than ever, I was in the inner circle. I went to parties where I was flanked by the people I saw in magazines, exotic sports cars, and celebrities. My business after a short, slow start, was taking off and we were gaining local notoriety. I have always felt very, very blessed, but wondered, what else is there? What is the next level now? What more could I want? How much more could success be judged by? Still the void was there taunting me.

After years of living the "good life" and "having it all"—a beautiful wife, two wonderful children, money, travel, nice cars, jewelry, etc.—a combination of greed, ego, misperception, addiction, and disconnection from gratitude yanked me from my world to a behavioral care facility. Okay, rehab. All of my success was stripped away and I was given a lot of time to think about my perception of success and what I thought success would give me. I looked at this exercise like a child creating his

Christmas list. This wasn't the Miss America Pageant; so, although I would love world peace, I decided to keep it personal.

I first thought **love**. Not adoration, but people who truly loved me. I figured I had a great family, my wife and kids tell me and show me regularly how much they love me, and I experience tangible expressions of their love. I cannot control how others perceive me, but the people who matter most love me. I checked off **love**.

The next on my list was **happiness**. Well, I have material stuff, I am breathing, and I have a family. Being happy is a personal choice. I am in total charge of how happy I wish to be. It is not out there, but it is inside of me. Why did this take so long to realize? It is my perception of things, people, and myself that allows me to label my life as being happy or not. I do not need things or external affirmation to be happy. Happiness? If I don't have it, I can get it. Check!

Health for my loved ones and me came to mind. At the time of writing this, all are healthy, under care, or on the mend. Health? Check!

My needs provided for. I realize now that after food, shelter, clothing, and security, everything else is gravy. If my transportation gets me to where I need to go, what the hood ornament represents is just ego fodder. Outside of being protected from the elements, the size of my house above and beyond its simple functional amenities should be considered a blessing. I know people who have rooms in their homes they never visit or occupy, while some in this world use a box for their entire dwelling if they even have one. Don't get me wrong. I enjoy life's perks as much as the next guy; it is just now not at the top of my priority pyramid. Needs? Check!

Presence. I wanted to enjoy the ride. I had spent so much time looking to the future, thinking "it" was all "out there." I know I missed many special moments, life's small victories, peaceful afternoons, personal reflections, and a lot of relaxation. I traded all of that for anticipation, anxiety, unrealistic expectations, and occasional dread. I heard people speak of presence, but I didn't listen or didn't understand. I was afraid I'd miss something—like the next rung of the ladder. Now I still plan my life and situations, but I stop to smell the roses and the coffee and the other stuff I'm supposed to smell. I hit cruise control and surrender to a will beyond my own. I am at peace with my journey and destination, and can be aware and appreciate all that occurs around me. Life is now more vivid and fulfilling and I realize I cannot deal with tomorrow until I get there. Presence? Check!

My list ended and it was shorter than I ever dreamed. I found if I was to expand the list it would reflect the old model of success—and that hadn't worked well for me. I had acquired things and still wanted more. My new list, this golden grail of what I wanted, the success I sought for the better part of my life, hit me as if someone had actually chucked the grail at my head. What I strove for all those years, those rungs in the ladder of success, didn't matter to me now. My old truths were no longer true to me.

Fulfilling? Yes! Appreciated? Absolutely! Am I grateful for what has happened in my life? Without a doubt! And no, I do not want to get rid of my toys, but I do have a new wish list. When I took the time to remove myself from the race, and truly and deeply reflect on what it was I wanted and what is important, I realized I had it and had it all along. At the very least I could have just reached for it.

I am now at a level of peace I have never felt or experienced before. I appreciate what I have, what I worked for, and the people around me. I see that things can be won or lost, as well as achieved and aspired to. The substance of what truly cultivates my soul and who I am and want to be is a much shorter list and is not as increasingly and perpetually elusive to me.

Simply put, everything I searched for was right under my nose. I just needed to open my eyes. I am blessed with abundance. I realize I have all I need. Everything else that comes along from here on out is just gravy!

I found this essay for me was simply coming to grips with "wanting what I have, not having what I want." I spent so much time valuing things and their representation of success. I thought once these barriers were breached, goals were attained, and things were gathered, that feeling of "having made it" would be bestowed upon me. I have heard, "he who dies with the most toys wins." I feel that "he, who dies with the most toys, is still dead and I've yet to see a U-Haul trailer behind a hearse." I have also never heard of any man on his deathbed explained, "Gee, I wish I spent more time at the office." My appreciation had to overtake my accumulation. When I look so far down the road, I lose sight of where I am and the ability to experience the blessings as they occur. Want and desire not only distract from living right now, but also pull us away and disconnect us from our ability to experience gratitude.

Reflections

Are there things I desire that never seem to materialize?

Do I feel as though my success is still out there?

Define "success" and what it means to me.

Do I have difficulty feeling thankful for where I am and what I have achieved?

Am I able to enjoy my life right now, or do I have a to-do list of things I must achieve first?

Am I waiting for something specific to happen or change to improve my life?

What would others say are my strengths and successes?

Do I feel like I have what I need, or do I feel that I need a lot more to be happy?

Why Not?

I don't mind being a "has-been," I just refuse to be a "never-was" as a result of succumbing to my own fears and apathy.

*To me, the fact that anyone is reading these words is a miracle. My writing, as well as a plethora of other desires and goals, have been postponed, shattered, and shunned by my biggest critic: me! Fear (**F**alse **E**vidence **A**ppearing **R**eal) and insecurity rented space in my head for so long I started to believe I did not deserve or live up to what was mine for the taking. I spooked myself, procrastinated, and then disappointed me and others. No longer will I allow fear to sabotage my potential.*

During my years in business, one passion of mine came to me by accident. While working for my father's company, we developed a symbiotic relationship with a local television affiliate, which at the time was one of the more visible stations in our market area. Long story short, our company, a large hair salon and day spa chain, would keep their on-air talent looking good, and in turn we would get our company logo posted at the end of the news broadcasts as well as the side bonus of a weekly, dedicated, on air spot where our company could do an informative piece on beauty and related topics. I was offered that position.

At first this was easy for a company of our size to generate points of interest in televised tidbits, as we were in-the-know and on-the-move as representatives of our industry. After a number of years of speaking around the country, I had a comfort zone in front of the camera, plus the ability to roll with the punches that came from many years of working on stage in front of a live audience. It came to me easy once I learned the rhythm, lingo, and on-air banter. My father always told me, "If bull sh** were snowflakes, you would be a blizzard!" I guess now I can capitalize on that.

The staff from the station not only became mentors, but my friends. I guess my ego got a stroke, but TV was just a new platform to get a message out to the masses, and that is what I also liked about being on the stage. Reaching the masses was simply a method of sharing information in digestible, approachable segments that real people could use. I wanted to be the local beauty liaison for the regular folks, and since I was very fortunate to get invited to see interesting places and things, I was able to share this information and the station saw value in what I had. In my career I have done approximately three hundred or so segments live on-air.

As coming up with fifty-two non-self-serving segments can be difficult, we reached a decision that allowed me, by my suggestion, to branch out into fields complimenting my expertise. I added health, fitness, anti-aging, as well as other charitable interests and a couple of random celebrity spots. It was nice to expand and share even more with the community. As my on-air presence increased, my visibility did as well. I decided to open my own company which allowed me more freedom to connect with our community. I loved being able to give a nod to local businesses, and I even gave time to local competitors as I always felt it was just the right thing to do. I think people also saw the integrity of sharing relevant information was my goal. This perception and TV presence really boosted my bottom line in my company early on. Many people came to see my business and I, to this day, still get random kind words from passersby. I became part of the TV station family, even though I was on the fringe, but I gained a passion for this medium as a way to share with others.

For many years I expressed a desire to host a TV show with a format that focused on celebrating people and their stories. Style, my forte, as well as beauty and wellness was the focus in the past, but now I wanted to add more to the mix than a simple three-minute segment on "How to trim your bangs at home." I don't care for the over-the-top programs that make the masses feel beauty is all on the exterior, fake, expensive, or unobtainable. I always felt there are more Columbus Ohio's than New York's and L.A.'s, so a "celebrity standard" for beauty was off-putting for me. I now wanted to create a lifestyle element with community events, family happenings, and things that improve the quality of one's life experience, such as dining out, music, and other enriching activities. This I would like to offer in a pleasing format that would engage viewers and connect people to our city and local personalities. Although I have friends in the media who have coached and mentored me, allowing me to slowly grow my dream into more than a passing thought—I still hesitated.

One day, a dear friend whom I truly love, and had met through the TV station years back, gave me advice on the subject. With his expertise in creating programs and an Emmy on his mantle, I consider him a valuable resource. He mentioned over our barber banter that he would like to help me on my goal of creating a TV show by taking on the role of temporary producer. He offered advice, script templates, mentoring, and potential coaching to get connected, and gave me some simple homework.

A couple weeks later I had a script template in hand, a connection, a direction, mentoring, and a deer-caught-in-the-headlights demeanor. It didn't seem real. I thought, "I cut hair for crying out loud! Who would want to watch me?" I didn't even think about the people that watched me over the years. I defaulted to my good buddies fear, insecurity, and procrastination. I found it is easier to come up with excuses than to forge ahead with my goal. I had sat on my dream for six years and knew this may be as close as I would get again.

Still, I would often hear myself say things like: "It's not for me", "I'm too old", "It's not what I do", "I can't afford to", "People will laugh at me", or "I will fail." I see now the paradox of procrastination is that it doesn't put failure off, it actually speeds it up. It starts the minute you slow down or stop working on your goals. It cuts out the middlemen of work, experience, and knowledge. I could spout any excuse, and get my brain to believe it in a couple seconds, as opposed to doing the work. Maybe I would be surprised; or maybe gain some new skills, or even meet a new mentor by accident. Maybe I would learn something I do not know, or God forbid I may achieve my dream!

The interesting and scary part is how rapidly my mind can shift to negative thoughts after such a positive meeting. How expensive will the show be? When will I possibly find the time? No one will watch! The excuses were endless.

The more I desired the dream, the more my ego and brain tried to destroy it. I was aware of the battle, but shaking it off was like escaping from a swarm of hornets. I could spend a good part of the day mourning the death of something I had not yet even given birth to!

What I realize now, is whenever I ask myself "Why me?" I should simply respond with "Why not me?" Something has placed the opportunity in front of me, so I need to carpe diem or "seize the day." The best thing I can do to achieve my dreams and receive what is rightfully mine is to realize that my mindset is a choice, the question of why or why not me is a choice, and acting on the intentions set in motion before me are a choice. Moving toward a goal can perhaps turn into failure, but not moving towards that goal insures failure. There is no reward without motion.

This fable exemplifies what I mean:

A man became trapped in his house during a flood. As the waters rose, his friends came frantically to his door, begging him to escape the torrent and to leave with them in their vehicles to insure survival. The man said, "I know God will rescue me, so I will stay here for now." As the waters rose, the man retreated to his upstairs and eventually found himself trying to survive on his roof as the water lapped at the gutters. A man in a modest rowboat came by, offering room in his boat, trying to save this man from a watery doom. The man denied the offer claiming, "I know God will rescue me, so I will wait here." The man in the boat paddled on. The water continued to rise and the weary man was clinging to the top of the chimney for his life. He noticed a helicopter overhead. The bullhorn bellowed, "Grab the rope we lowered! We will pull you aboard! Save yourself!" The man yelled back, "I know God will rescue me, so I will wait here!" The coaxing was to no avail and the helicopter left. Sadly, the man drowned. Upon entering heaven, he was greeted at the pearly gates by God. After all, he was a man of strong faith and conviction. The man asked God, "God, I pray to you. I serve you, and stayed in the water knowing you would eventually help me, yet you didn't; how come?" God replied, "What did you want? I sent your friends, a boat, and a helicopter!"

We must be able to see opportunity. We must be receptive. We have to take risks, leaps of faith, and finally, we have to know we have God's support. At least, that is what gets me by and gives me strength.

I am at peace with whatever happens, but I have to allow it to happen by engaging my personal steps down the path toward my goal. I have to take risks in order to enjoy the journey. When doors are opened for us, we still must walk through them. I've always heard "nothing ventured, nothing gained" and believe it now as something more than fortune-cookie wisdom.

The book that you hold in your hand is not only the journal of one man's excursion toward personal growth; it is also my remedy of trying to right the wrongs of my old procrastinating ways. My first declaration of desiring to write a book was in 1991. It is now 2009. No more! Maybe this book will make it to bookstore shelves and maybe my show will come into fruition on a station someday. No matter the situation; in the future instead of saying "Why me", I will only say "Why not me?" I don't mind being a has-been, but I don't want to be a never-was.

---

*In moments of doubt I am reminded I need to believe in myself as others do, but also I need to use my tools of faith and patience. I have to believe in that which I do not see, and also accept that perhaps **right now** is not the best time for what I desire to occur. I have heard the saying "It is better to have loved and lost than to never have loved at all." I will hold on to my version: "It is better to have tried and failed than to never have tried at all."*

There are many people out there who attempt to tell us why something shouldn't happen or won't happen, but I see now I do not have to support or entertain their opinions.

Reflections

Do I try to defeat myself before I even start something?

Do I experience fear when striving for or dreaming about my goals?

Do I feel unworthy or ask "why me?"

Do I feel unqualified or question my skills when trying something new?

Do I procrastinate or not finish things that are important to me?

Do I let myself and others down when I do this?

What is preventing me from achieving my dreams?

Do I see the strengths in me that others recognize?

Quite The Experience

Gratitude occurs the moment I realize I am blessed; most often beyond my current deserving.

*My confusion and curiosity on the subject of gratitude was stirred by the similarity and yet separateness of the words "thankful" and "grateful." I always felt one was more intense than the other and that one was **practiced** while the other was a **deeper experience**. This essay is my interpretation of these principles. I invite you to reflect on your personal interpretation as well.*

Probably the words parents drill the most into their children, save "mama" and "dada", are "thank you." As soon as infant fingers unfurl to receive food and toys we prompt them to say thank you. We prompt our children with incessant obsession, encouraging them to be polite, conform to our social etiquette requirements, and to acknowledge when they have received something. From an early age, we are given Cheerios on our highchair, and are told, "Say thank you!" Over time we Mynah bird back, "thank you" in some utterance close enough to please our parents. We receive a piece of gum, we are told: "Say thank you." Someone hands you a pen: "Say thank you." Someone holds the door for you: "Thank you." Perhaps they mention, "You look nice today!" —"Why, thank you!" It goes on and on. It is a courtesy, but also to the giver, it is a requirement to alleviate a degree of potential offense for lack of acknowledgment of the transaction. How many times have you heard "They didn't even say thank you?"

As a kid I was still reminded to express it to my great-grandmother, God rest her soul, as she would innocently present my cousin and I with onesie pajamas that had the feet in them. The prompting came from our parents as our disappointment was apparent. Nana was in "her own place" at that point. We were in our young teens hoping for a card that contained cash. Good upbringing made me aware that to stay in good graces, to please others, and just because it was right. "Thank you" should always be at the ready—and better too often than not enough. Upon reflection, I realize I can say thank you in Spanish, French, Japanese, Russian, German, and Italian. No, I don't speak those languages fluently but this shows that "thank you" is a global requirement.

Now, what brings me to this essay is more than an evaluation of the usage of the words "thank you." I wanted to explore gratitude. I am familiar with the vocal exchange of "thank you," as well as giving thanks, being thankful, Thanksgiving, and many variations, but after hearing more about gratitude recently, I decided to examine what the two meant to and for me. Aside from the gratuitous expression of the words "thank you", I was aware of its prevalence in my life. I was thankful I had enough gas to make it to work. I am thankful my kids remembered to get me a Father's Day card. I am thankful I have enough money to pay my bills. I am thankful I still have some hair. I am thankful I can read and write. I could go on infinitely, but I thought, "isn't gratitude and thankful interchangeable?"

So I went to my trusty search engine and typed, "thankful + definition", and "grateful + definition" in the small rectangular box of wisdom of all things Internet. To my dissatisfaction, similar outcomes in the definitions exclaimed, "aware and appreciative of a benefit", and "expressive of gratitude" as being the most common results in my research. Without desiring to debate, I found the terms "thankful" and "grateful" were interchangeable acts of acknowledgment and appreciation of a benefit. I will also add, to also acknowledge that a transaction occurred.

Recently, I have come across hearing of gratitude more frequently. From religious to recovery discussions, gratitude is part of the golden recipe that is taught as a paramount component to many things positive, including emotional stability, spirituality, and even good physical health.

Thankfulness is a result of a positive transaction, idle pleasantries, a benefit received, manners exchanged, and both parties are better for the experience. Gratitude, on the other hand, is totally different for me. First, the feeling is unexpected. I can't go searching for it, attempt to write it down, or try to hold gratitude; it just washes over me and occurs unpredictably. Second, gratitude is powerful and endures. I don't easily forget gratitude and I feel overwhelmed with emotion—in some cases moved to tears or I get chills. Third, gratitude feels like a gift, a gift I oftentimes feel I am lucky or even unworthy to receive. It is like a gift from the heavens that makes me richer for having been a part of it. Finally, I find gratitude is an experience of a spiritual nature that no transaction had to occur for me to receive. It is not part of an action, but rather an amazing feeling often found accompanying love on some level.

I can actively participate in things while being thankful. It is something I do. I look for opportunities, and I practice it. Being in gratitude however, is a state for me. I cannot necessarily reach for gratitude as much as be prepared to receive it. The preparation is an awareness of my blessings, staying connected in my spiritual state, and being present, as well as being thankful. It is being open and receptive to the experience.

I am thankful I have friends, but I am grateful when I experience their love. I am thankful for a home for my family and me, but am grateful when I recognize my life's path has provided me with the blessings of abundance. I am thankful to be healthy, sober, and alive, but I am grateful for the experience of clarity, and ability to be touched by life on such a deep level. I am thankful for beautiful, happy, wonderful people in my family; I am grateful upon realization they are such wonderful components to my being and key players in my life story.

Again, these are my observations and they helped me separate the two and respect them individually: thankful, being an act or a practice, and gratitude being a state. They can exist together or exclusively in any point in time. Thankfulness, although it can be fleeting, is no less important, but gratitude, I have found, embeds itself deeper as a part of my core being. It changes me.

Hume once wrote: "A deficiency in this feeling is a failing so severe as to be of all crimes that human beings are capable of committing, it is the most horrid and unnatural." I am thankful I discovered this before it's too late and grateful that I am able to share it!

I knew to move onward in my personal journey, I had to figure out how to tune in and experience the blessings of a state of gratitude. I can feel when gratitude is in me. It is like a Divine sector of my emotional being has been unlocked and allowed to totally dominate a specific moment in time. I find it as potent as love, in essence it is. It calls me to embrace and devour the message I am receiving.

Gratitude occurred to me only after I ceased looking for what I wanted, and started enjoying what I had. I asked to be shown and shared with, and to connect to the blessings in my life. I found they are not hidden, they are present and awaiting their turn to materialize for all of us. I am in awe at what has been revealed to me. It is like putting on a pair of 3-D glasses: what has been there all along is much more crisp and clear, pronounced, dimensional, and available to experience. It is like life in high-def.

Reflections

Are being thankful and grateful the same thing to you? Why or why not?

Am I grateful? Have I experienced true gratitude?

If yes, when did it happen and what did gratitude feel like?

Is this feeling of gratitude temporary or enduring? Explain.

What does being thankful or grateful do for me?

Is it is easy or difficult to experience these?

Can I feel grateful when things are not going my way?

List a few things I am thankful for.

Did or does a feeling of gratitude change me; if so, how?

It's An As-Is Deal

People spend more time contemplating love than simply expressing it!

I see love as spiritual superglue. Love can bond us to others as well as ourselves, and it potentially allows us to forgo judgment and other acts of separation that are counterproductive. Love does not always need to operate within the confines of what people interpret as a "relationship", but can grow and be experienced in various ways. This way we do not have to necessarily wait on others to enable love's magic. We can exist at any moment in a state of love and reap the emotional and physical benefits. There are a variety of principles of love to which we all can connect. I have found a greater abundance of love waiting to be realized and shared, and because of that my life became richer.

My most recent contemplation has been on a topic I adore and that frightens me equally: love. Outside of perhaps religion, sex, and politics, love can be controversial and generate many interpretations. I am by no means a professional on the subject. I just wish to share a few of my observations on the topic. They were not picked by me, but more so placed in front of me as part of my personal evolution.

I decided to avoid types of love that may be subjective, personal, and not my place to decipher or define. Let's look at happiness for example, you can say "happy" in a general way, but are we talking happy as in the context of, "I am so happy I just hit the lotto", or "I am happy I found my soul mate", even "I am happy that they are playing Cosby show reruns tonight", to "I am happy that she is out of my life?" What I have examined here is that love can take as many forms as happiness.

Whenever I or others have had conflict, I have found we can easily default to looking for a loss, a void, or absence of love. Children often state for example, "You don't love me anymore." "He must not love me", could perhaps be exclaimed in a domestic squabble. Or, "God doesn't love me", when things don't always go our way. How about the classic, "nobody loves me", when we decide to feel like we are a victim, and it is us against the world? It seems that we often feel that love is bestowed upon us; and in a cosmic punishment can be yanked from us. Therefore we can feel our worth and value diminish when this happens. We may feel if it is not given or released to us, we suffer. Our ego can allow us to attach our worth to receiving love, and without it, we feel our stock drops, we devaluate, and our worth plummets. We may even exclaim, "How can I even now be worthy of love, to have once loved, then lost it?"

There is a large misconception of love being an exclusive property of relationships, like when used in the context of "I am in love!" Many believe love requires two or more people for love to exist, and to be pure and good, it must be reciprocated. They may feel that an equal exchange is required for love to work. The problem is each person has a unique, fluctuating, and varying standard of what love is. Since love is subject to personal interpretation, it is hard to find two people whose views match perfectly. How can one's love mirror another's? They can be similar of course, equally passionate, most certainly; but one is not necessary to fuel the other or to be present for it to exist.

You can love exclusively. Love does not require another's acceptance or validation or even awareness to be able to survive. A relationship requires that in most cases, but love in and of itself does not. I find when I selfishly need another's returned love or acceptance it changes my perception and the dynamic. Is equal and returned love nice to have? Absolutely! Is it necessary for me to be able to love? No.

My next observation was that to receive love from others, whether it is romantic or even brotherly, or by any degree for that matter, I had to be "loveable" or "able to be loved." I must be compassionate and aware of the gift of love others can bestow upon me and receive it as it is: a true gift. Try to receive love from others in a manner that you wish others would receive yours. How would I feel if someone met my love, either shown or verbally expressed, with dismissal, sarcasm, indifference, anger, control, or without any value? I would most likely be hurt, my spirit bruised, and I would question my desire to love again, which often happens. Remember you don't have to love someone back to be loved, but you will shut yourself down from love's energy. Shutting down your receptiveness in any way denies you the full potential of love's energy and one of life's greatest gifts. Be open to love, even if not in a relationship. You don't have to throw down the welcome mat, just don't lock the door!

Finally, like happiness, you have to have love in order to give it. It must exist within you to be able to show it or to share it. You can wait for someone to give it to you, or for someone to allow you to experience love, but then you run the risk of forever searching in a void. You can choose to love at any moment instantaneously! You must, however, start by loving yourself! There is no personal fault so great, no character or physical flaw so appalling, nothing in your past so horrific that you cannot choose to forgive and forget, or at least forgive and work on it when it comes to self-love. Your love of self can happen right now; it is your choice to activate it! Right now, and I mean right now, you can say, "I love me for who I am." And that should include the whole package. There is no other being on the planet who you can spontaneously approach at this instant, and command "Love me!" and get the response of "Okay!" as easily as you can to yourself.

I spent a long time thinking to love myself was foolish and that if no one else loved me how could I love me? But now I realize, I can simply say, "I love myself," and can practice loving myself accordingly. It helps me to see and experience love from others as again, and to see that love has many forms. So whether you are currently in love or looking for love in a relationship; work on the loving relationship that is easiest and most important in your life and that relationship is being able to love yourself initially.

What helps me love myself and others is to understand that love is an unconditional acceptance of one's unique nature **as-is**! I do not have to like every part of someone (or myself), rather I need to understand that every component—from their engaging laugh, to their romantic expressions, to their snore, or to the fact they don't like pizza—are all part of the whole package. Even in cases of opposing personalities or estrangement, we don't have to like everything but rather accept everything. Compromises are necessary for harmony in relationships. When love exists, compromise must be sought to enrich the relationship. Where love is to exist, the **as-is** clause is critical. Let go of the past and remember to focus on and love your present self.

Appreciate the positives in yourself and others. It is imperative to remember that the acceptance you hope others will bestow upon you in your faults, quirks, and eccentricities, you must in turn show upon others. In giving and receiving love, no matter its form, it is an as-is deal.

---

*You can evoke love's presence and power at any given moment. Love allows you to connect with others on a higher spiritual level, and puts you in a position, or state, that helps you attract love in return. Loving as many as possible nourishes your soul and makes it difficult for the emergence of ego and judgment in your life. With that, the element of accepting others **as-is**, is heightened to where you do not disconnect as quickly or easily when confronted with words or actions different from yours.*

I have noticed my overall stress level is monumentally reduced. I notice fewer faults in others where I used to be judgmental. I can accept that which I may not like or disagree with, and I notice I am more accepting of others and more forgiving of myself. I feel now that if I can love myself, perhaps others can and will. I have a sense of peace I never felt towards others and myself, and embrace the love and let live mantra.

Reflections

Is it easy for me to love myself? How about others?

Do I need to receive love before I can give love?

Do I have strong criteria I hold people to before I extend my love?

Is it difficult for me to accept differences in others? If yes, does it affect my ability to love people?

Do I love myself; if not, what is holding me back?

Do I love people as individuals in their own way, or am I a one-love-fits-all believer?

When I am hurt, do I pull love from all areas and persons even if they were not involved?

Letting It Go

What other people do is a testimony to their character. How we respond is a testimony to ours.

*It used to be easy for me to choose my battles. Why, because I chose them all. What is it in us at times that desires to embrace conflict? What is the magnetism that not only allows us to gravitate to conflicts, but to hold onto and to replay the situations long after the occurrence? I often wonder where that threshold is between just letting things roll off, and to where we decide to put on the blue "Braveheart" war paint on our face, raise our swords, and shout the battle cry that "it's go time!" For me, it was not so much a battle over the validity of my truth, as it was my opinion of the **incorrectness** of another's personal truth. My ego desired that I not only stand behind my truth, but also **convert** the other person and replace his or her viewpoints with my own. I no longer have the need to fight or argue to prove myself. My truth is just that: my own.*

    Recently I have noticed that I am less likely to react negatively to something when I am in the presence of a conflict. A true redneck at heart, I pride myself on my small-town roots and I do not use the term "redneck" disparagingly. Some of the greatest people I have ever known, songs I've heard, food I have eaten, company I have kept, and wisdom I have acquired, has come from my redneck brethren. I refer here more to the qualities of a down-home sense of fun, the ability to do more with less, and to go toe-to-toe over what I believe in.

    I always loved a good scrap. I was never so much a fighter, even with my weapons and hand-to-hand combat training. I was never a beast of a man and I always knew that the bar room training of a good 'ole boy redneck can create a formidable opponent of one who was trained in a dojo. My weapon of choice was often my wit. I was in most cases a clown, but if I decided to take off the rubber nose and start in on at battle of the sharp tongue, I could be a worthy opponent. I would try to dominate any argument at all costs. I always said I loved a battle of the wits with an unarmed opponent.

I eventually grew beyond the "meet me behind the dugouts" type of confrontation. I could always revert to martial skills if needed, but I found intellectualizing, using guilt, shame, or simply manipulating situations to make myself appear the victim became the new chosen tactic. I used to replay conflicts in my head for hours, analyzing them as a football commentator might. I would think "if only I would have said this instead of that," or "if only I had done or said something more noble and with valor I could have dominated." I wanted to save face, even if no one was around to see what happened. I wanted to win, and to win like there were cute girls watching. "Suckers lose, fools compromise, unless of course they receive something in return," I often thought. I would also think, "Who does this person think they are, expressing their opinion to me?" Don't they know they have now disrespected me and we must now fight to the death? This concept works for samurai and gangs, why not me?

Now however, instead of preparing for battle, I ask myself, "How true is this information? How long do I wish to drag out this conflict and how enduring do I desire it to be? Does it truly affect me mentally or physically, or am I inviting something in and creating a painful scenario?" I also evaluate how much of my personal power I am willing to invest in this person, with the loss of it being at my expense.

Recently I was enjoying a conversation with my wife at our pool club, while our son played with the some kids in the shallow end of the pool. We hadn't been there long before a strange gentleman approached us, dripping wet in his swim trunks. He proceeded to inform us that our son was encroaching upon his space while he was playing with his own son. He felt our boy was disturbing them by trying to invite himself in to their bonding moment. While telling us this, the man was fidgety and had trouble making eye contact. He proceeded to give his non-professional opinion that he felt our son was "lonely"—in a roundabout way he was offering his talk-show variety parenting advice in a quick sound bite. After a couple minutes, he walked away. Shocked, neither my wife nor I responded. We were momentarily speechless. All the while he spoke to us, I remained seated, kept a cordial smile, and my wife reclined next to me. I did not notice her expression or demeanor, as I was fixated on the "sermon."

After his exit, and a moment of shocked silence, my wife expressed how appalled she was and wondered what she or we should do. I stated, "If you are worried about what that guy thinks, you can get in the pool with our son to show him what a wonderful mom you are." She remained angry and was understandably and temporarily without further words. She asked how I felt. I said, "He's a coward, and I prefer to never give a fool an audience." She couldn't believe my response, but it was what I felt at the time. (What she doesn't know was that twenty years of studying Bruce Lee's moves did indeed prompt some responses to run through my head; like visions of kicking his sternum through his spine and then urinating on his motionless body floating face down in the pool while I made rude comments about his mother; which had come and since passed thankfully.) I realize my old behavior would have taken an untrue statement from a random stranger and manifested it into a physical confrontation. It possibly would have resulted in someone getting hurt, our family kicked out of the club, embarrassment for my family, a bad example for our kids, a possible arrest, and on and on. As I said, the man had trouble making eye contact and was visibly uncomfortable. Perhaps he was prompted to approach us by someone else. I don't know. What I do know is that I can control me and what I think and do.

I moved to a shady spot for a while to read and then ventured to the "Snack Shack" with my son. I was happy to see that he appeared to not be suffering from any loneliness. About an hour later I returned to my wife's side. Her disgust over the confrontation had gained momentum. She had recruited reinforcement as she shared the incident with a friend. My wife gave a detailed account of what happened to her friend and offered a couple proposed outcomes. She asked me to recall a small detail of what was said and it took me a second to remember. I had moved on and simply dismissed the incident. I exclaimed, "You're still on that guy?!" She snarled, "YES!" as if she was surprised I was not plotting on how to get him in the parking lot.

My wife exclaimed that she was upset we did not say anything; which may have been justified, but we were caught off guard and shocked at the time. And I also thought to myself, "To what benefit would saying anything do? Was it worth turning a thirty-second monologue from a random guy at the pool into a full-on redneck smack down?" (Maybe. Okay, maybe not.)

My wife and her friend dug up some dirt as to the true identity of our drive-by child psychologist. They found through public opinion he was lacking in social graces in other situations, and has been found guilty of other intolerable infractions, so we were not the only sufferers. I mentioned that maybe he was a "serial asshole", again not helping my situation.

Hours later, when the subject resurfaced, my wife and I came to a mutual understanding on the matter: our ownership of what we can control in ourselves determines our happiness, as well as the outcome and duration of most conflicts we encounter regardless of the circumstance. We can choose to let it go. How mad we get and for how long are up to us, and I chose to save my spinning side kick for a more deserving victim. I know she has since moved on, probably hasn't forgotten, and that is okay. I think we both grew a bit in all this. I admit my recall in writing this did put up a fleeting fantasy of putting a UFC choke hold on the guy until he needed an adult diaper, and that's not healthy now is it? I still need work.

Forgiveness is an essential component in my stability in any confrontational situation. I realize I do not need to hear "I'm sorry" to be able to say "I forgive you." I love the quote "Forgiveness is the fragrance the violet leaves behind upon the heel that crushed it." I notice the sooner I forgive the indiscretions and differences without defaulting to verbal attacks or physical violence, the better I feel. I also have to forgive myself, and my ownership as instigator and recipient of any repercussions. Once I could forgive myself for my actions, or inactions, my humanity, and any exchanges I would make whether proper or improper, I found I was closer to closure. I could then forgive the others involved knowing that I was only harboring ill-will and trying to control the uncontrollable. I now avoid digging up my expectations or resentments I have of others and myself, which both are only my ego's desire to control others according to my plan, or perceptions of how they should perform for me.

I have learned to forgive what I used to perceive were unforgivable infractions upon me or mine. I forgive and deal with what is in front of me now. When conflict does arise, I know I am in control of what I can do or say, the way I choose to let it affect me, the labels I place upon it, and the duration of its effect upon me.

Of course I get mad, and of course I do not like it. Yes, my feelings get bruised, but now my awareness of how I own my own stuff is vital to my recovery. Likewise, you must remember you cannot control others and their reality any more than they can control yours.

Often we encounter situations where we find we are on the same planet but different worlds with others. That is okay! We do not need to keep hitting the rewind button to keep finding more ways to feel violated within the same situation. We can arm ourselves with the simple questions like: "Is it true", and "whose truth is it?" "Does this truly affect me in any tangible way?" "Is this conflict enduring, or I am I feeding it my energy?" Also, "How much power am I willing to give this person or situation?" I have come to realize these questions are a good filter for me and the awareness helps me digest things in a healthier way. I am still a redneck at heart, so there are times when I find myself asking this simple question: "What would Chuck Norris do?"

We've all heard an elementary solution to this dilemma: "Sticks and stones may break my bones, but words will never hurt me!"* Interestingly, we will empower simple, benign words and elevate them to have the destructive ability to equal that of sticks and stones. I notice if I choose to smile and nod, even in the case of extreme disagreement, **my** *truth does not have to change within me when challenged by another.*

Often I see in many cases where my personal serenity and calm demeanor will diffuse the challenger's will to where they often cease action or back down. Perhaps it is because it is no fun to battle alone, or maybe it is a testimony to my own comfort in my beliefs that the fight seems futile. I do not know, but if I ask myself the questions I mentioned above, I can determine whether or not to respond, in what manner, and at what cost or gain.

I also try to quickly examine if it is simply my ego trying to replace another's truth with my own. Quite often, the methods we use to try to be right or to replace another's view with our own is more volatile and damaging than simply smiling and letting it go. You must realize that your state or truth does not have to suffer or change upon the whims or opinions of others.

* My mother-in-law offered me an alternative to this. In working for an elementary school for many years she said this variation to the children: "Stick and stones can break my bones, but words can break my heart." Thanks Sharon!

Reflections

Am I quick to anger or argue when my views are challenged?

Is it easy or difficult for me to "agree to disagree"?

If I do not defend myself against another's challenge of my viewpoint, do I feel it is a sign of weakness or strength?

When I choose "battle mode," do I feel better or worse after it is over?

Will others see strength in me if I choose peaceful positions and silence as opposed to heated engagement?

Others have the right to opinion as much as I do, and the perception of the truth in any matter can vary between people. True or false?

Before engaging in debate, am I able to take a deep breath and momentarily think through something to see if the debate itself causes more harm than good?

Am I able to be silent when challenged to maintain peace with those around me, even if I feel I am right?

Please Don't Change

People like predictability, especially in the behavior of those closest to them.

*Being different is okay. I spent so many years trying to fit in, but now I wonder, "Fit into what?!" I think there is not so much **serenity** as there is **security** in conforming. By trying to fit in to an external mold that is often imposed upon us, we start down this perpetual path of people-pleasing –often forsaking ourselves, our desires, or our dignity. We are taught at a young age that just because someone else does something, we do not have to follow in suit; yet, on the other hand, we are told to do what others do and to do what is expected of us. It must be confusing to kids, as it confuses me now.*

Aside from rules that keep society from anarchy and in proper stride, I find at times a lot of us find our uniqueness creates fear in others, and brings judgment on us. I have heard terms like "nutty professor", or "hopeless romantic" attached by others to describe ones' actions as being odd. The titles are usually given when someone deviates from an expected pattern of thought or behavior.

*I have often experienced conflict in my desire to be true to myself, my internal belief system, at the risk of appearing "insane" to others. When I have appeared most crazy to others, is when I am most **inspired,** or when I am doing what I feel compelled or called to do. Is it insanity or visionary? Some of our greatest inventors, pioneers, and saviors broke away from the social molds and parameters others placed around them. Only then did they excel and evolve into their true potential and experience peace knowing they did what they had to do at the risk of losing favor, falling from grace, or appearing insane.*

I remember the times in high school where my friend Mike and I used to pass sheets of paper back and forth in our psych class. This clandestine paper often contained doodles, thoughts, and random snippets that just seemed to pop into our bored minds. We would often share deep thoughts and observations. Sometimes it would be an obscure exercise of word association where each pass from person to person would add a word to the others' previous entry. Ultimately, a very random and ridiculous creation would spark stifled laughter. I remember now getting A's and B's in the subject matter but horrible conduct grades for my desire to add my perspective to the curriculum, and yes my perspective was unsolicited.

What I liked about Mike was that he was intelligent and a kind soul and got along with about anyone. He was artistic, musically talented, creative and funny. We had many similarities in our sense of humor, and that is where we bonded.

Our little written daily exchanges, at least for me, allowed me to be strange, yet understood, and enjoyed by another who could spend time with me in my silly world without feeling alien. I found very few allies, as if you were not an athlete, achiever, or an academic, being a dreamer or an artist could mark you for a bully's target. My wit and sense of humor bonded me with the jocks as well as the knuckleheads, and I look back and I see that I could easily be the social chameleon at a moment's call.

One day, Mike and I sat at our desks and awaited the day's topic of our writings to pop into our heads or any pearls of wisdom for that matter. I nudged Mike with the folded paper intending to get him to start a thread. With the two of us, anything, and I mean anything could start us into an exchange that would cause the school counselors to debate between our brilliance and our insanity. Mike passed the fresh sheet of notebook paper to me, folded in the usual top to bottom fashion, and with the typical required sleight of hand. I received it and read. The words written have since remained with me as a favorite quote of mine, and since I know not of the origin, I will credit my friend Mike. The words touched me and have been a mantra of mine ever since. The words were as follows: "In a world of insane people, the sole sane person seems insane." Thanks Mike!

Through the next couple decades I did find that uncovering life's true meaning had remained a priority for me. Sadly though, it became like a photo you keep in your wallet that gets shuffled and lost in the random stuff. It was never gone, just partially forgotten and fully buried.

I liked pleasing people, and at times to a fault. I spent a lot of time seeking love, confirmation, affirmation, and acceptance from people who were never going to give it to me. I realize now that my standards and desires clashed with what others thought I should be. I modeled success not on my standards and soul's desire, but by the material and emotional standards of others. It was drilled into me that one doesn't dream; but you are to achieve goals. Being introspective and working on personal growth is a waste of time and "self-help mystic mumbo-jumbo." It was often misinterpreted by those around me, and was considered "lazy" and a "waste of time." In my career I have been often accused of not being "confrontational enough", "not hard enough", "weak", and a "bad leader" to name a few. These taunts often came from people with apparent high blood pressure, continual frustration, and their own personal problems in my opinion. I always felt I can sleep at night, and I at least try to treat others as I wish to be treated. Somewhere between the two is probably the correct place to be.

Over the years, I tried things their way. The results left me suffering, thirstier, and unfulfilled. I thought I had to achieve by selling my soul to a career, acquire the required things, and provide for a family by sacrificing a lot of my own desires. Those things I indeed did and some degree of satisfaction had surfaced; yet my spiritual cancer worsened. To spare insignificant details, the shift started: family estrangement, material loss, relationship strain, self-doubt, and eventually substance abuse landed me for an extended stay in a rehab facility. Broken, bitter, and scared, I entered my cocoon to later emerge transformed. I will now fast forward.

After completing treatment, I reentered the world refreshed but somewhat fragile. I had a newfound spiritual rejuvenation, sobriety tools, and a desire to show the world the new me. Unfortunately, I found the same world and the same obstacles waiting patiently, ready to test my new resolve. The same standards and expectations were still present. I was not reaching them according to the world's terms. I quickly learned I could not simply explain my thoughts, feelings, and intentions, but had to actually live them for others to see. I had to physically manifest the changes. I didn't like this, as in the past, I was not known for being a pillar of patience. I saw it now as imperative to spiritual growth and inner peace. I constantly had to work on the acceptance of others as well as to gain favor in their opinions, viewpoints, and traditions, especially when I was in their presence.

I tried to understand as opposed to intellectualize, and I tried to avoid the need to be right. I had to realize it would take time, and that if I were to ever be who I wanted to be, and be okay with me, I had to really work at it. I had to have happiness to share it.

I knew what I wanted was out there waiting, and I was going to go for it. I read books, attended support groups, watched DVDs, prayed, and meditated. I feasted on, and devoured any information I could. I did not follow any specific person or tome at this point, but relied on the Divine to take me where I should go. From the mystical to Biblical, yoga and diet, and other tools, I sought a new place. I felt great! Others mentioned that I seemed like a new man. I felt better being in my own skin.

The biggest realization I find is, as one changes in the nature that I feel I have, it is quite quantum in scope. My entire value system changed; my perceptions changed–life changed. I get joyous or emotional over things that used to disappear before me, or perhaps never even presented themselves. And my expressions have been called "silly" or "weird." Since the great ego-deflation, material goods and titles of achievement are not as important as they once were. I still enjoy my toys, and I want them in my life to enjoy abundance, but I prefer these things as rewards for service as opposed to selfish desires in and of themselves or for public acceptance.

Some people have become confused because I no longer fit into the mold they once had cast for me. I have found people like to be able to predict the behavior of those in their lives, both the positive and negative. I can almost hear, "Please don't change. Stay the same conforming, miserable, person you were, as it makes you more predictable to all of us!" I used to subscribe to this mentality as well. Happy people were no fun to bitch to. They always looked for that blasted bright side as opposed to bringing their own tales of woe that would validate to all in ear shot that what we were feeling was correct, and that we were right in harboring resentments.

As I alienated some people, I gained new friends. I realize I am not nor ever have to be alone, and that in itself is a blessed feeling. Only the awakened know they are awake, and it is a joy to see the light come on. I know it is easier to remain the same than to evolve. The hard part is that to change is to often appear insane.

I guess that is why the quote my high-school buddy Mike passed to me one day in psych class years ago has remained so poignant: "In a world of insane people, the sole sane person seems insane!" I guess

I don't mind the insanity. I have experienced the other kind, the real kind. Where I am now feels much better to me. I am still growing, and still evolving, but I have a new understanding, gratitude, and appreciation for life. If this is insanity, I will gladly wait for everyone here at the asylum.

Occasionally, I have incidents where my actions appear foreign or threatening to others. I wrestle with the fact that I may be causing unintentional fear and unrest in them and bring judgment upon myself. Then, I remind myself that I cannot, nor ever will be able to control their thoughts or reactions, especially if I choose to be and remain true to myself.

I can lead by example and embrace others' unique quirks and viewpoints. I can abstain from superficial judgments especially without grounds or facts to support my criticisms. I can also choose to seek something I actually appreciate in others as a point of connection in which to bond. I do not have to make these blanketing or global judgments or assumptions presuming someone to be weird, different, unlovable, unapproachable, or unwelcome in my world. I have noticed the more I have tried to eliminate fear and judgment through love and understanding, the more I feel loved and understood.

I now celebrate my individuality and seek to celebrate it in others. I have traded my self-perception and fear of apparent insanity to the embrace of individuality within myself. If I am eventually put in a straitjacket, at least I will forever be in a position to hug myself.

Reflections

Have I ever felt different from others? How does this make me feel?

When following my passions or calling, do I get encouragement or judgment?

Do people appreciate the quirks that make me, me? Do they find them endearing or threatening?

When I find myself going against the norm, do I feel energized or paralyzed?

What holds me back from doing, saying, or feeling what I truly believe?

When I am being myself, do I feel alone?

Do I need approval from others before I act on something?

What will it take for me to find comfort with myself and to feel blessed by my uniqueness?

Alone In A Crowd

Peaceful solitude and agonizing loneliness often teeter on our *perception* of a situation.

Have you ever felt alone or lonely? These words are powerful in how they cause an emotional reaction within us, recall memories, and remain with us. They can cause us to suffer in one form or another. There are plenty of alternatives to turn to when feeling alone or lonely. First we must decipher what we are feeling and why. Only then can we experience the motivation we need to move forward, as well as to find a healthy connection to replace or dissipate that which is draining to us. The upside to being alone is we are less subjected to the outside opinions of whom and what we should become.

"Mid-life crisis, I consider it more of a 'Mid-life awakening!" My definition of a crisis is an undesirable event or circumstance, in which the main goal is to recover manageability of the situation, and to arrive at a desired outcome. Recently, I have felt that I could be perceived as having a mid-life crisis. I do not however, intend to purchase a shiny sports car; I do enjoy my family and feel fulfilled, and I have not started dressing below my years, (although I did recently opt for a tattoo of an ambigram of my kid's names on my wrist.) To let you in on a secret though, I honestly wish I had some of my hair back.

In addition, I have not had revelations of seeing death creep towards me at a more progressive or frenetic pace. I am not frightened by a feeling that time is fleeting. I also do not feel as if I have to go back through my boyhood dreams and scratch off what my adolescent self did not get around to. Aside from occasional desires of the hair and vitality of my twenties, I feel pretty good!

What I noticed when looking back to make some sense of where I am now, I see that any time I had a conflict, either internal or external, I would feel alone. Not lonely per se, (except for an occasional relationship hiccup here and there,) as I never really subscribed to feeling there was no one out there for me. With billions of people on the planet, I figured I eventually had a shot. Lonely, to me, was more of an unfulfilled desire to be around others. I am a social person, so my feelings of being lonely were either a choice or short-lived which didn't hinder me long. There is always someone to socialize or connect with if you simply try: from jobs, churches, restaurants, clubs, online social networks, etc. You almost have to try to be lonely. Often loneliness occurs after a loss or void in one's life, and yes, can take you into an emotional dip; but I see loneliness, in and of itself, is rarely terminal, chronic, or fatal.

Alone, on the other hand, is something completely different. Being alone can cause you to believe you do not need a connection, or you perpetually choose isolation to where it becomes a familiar and oddly comforting pattern. I felt most alone when I was being misunderstood. I believe sometimes the loneliest place is in a crowd.

A crowd lends itself to a dynamic of a collaborative understanding. It represents a socially created consciousness that works for the group culture. Individuals must fit into it and blend. This often starts in early adolescence with cliques, sports, and social organizations; where even schools often prove that when to feel, think, or act uniquely can cause one to be ostracized. Sometimes teasing, bullying, and even physical violence, is displayed to where one still may feel as they always have, but become afraid to share, in fear of being unaccepted for their views and eccentricities.

This often caused me to internalize my opinions and has made it difficult for me to find like-minded people and kindred spirits in the past. I would settle alone in my dream space, feeling misunderstood. I also noticed the yellow alert from those around me when they saw I had changed. My subsequent withdrawal from their presence caused suspicion, scrutiny, speculation, and mistrust. I have been accused of many things from being depressed to infractions of infidelity, simply because I started to desire new and different experiences in my life.

At the age of forty-four, I want to take yoga and talk with old high-school chums online. This should not be cause for alarm. It does not mean I'm going to sell my belongings to runaway with an Argentinean model to do braids on the beach in a seaside hut. It means

I am older and want to be more limber, and I enjoy talking with old friends whom I have not seen in years. Nothing more, but these new endeavors threaten the integrity of the social mold I dwelled in for many years. I understand the fears, and must respect that the changes in me have not occurred in those around me.

Once we challenge the old norm, the resulting alarm can cause a desire within us to stifle our dreams and any future proclamations of them to others. This stifling and isolation at first can cause boredom, and can evolve into resentment. We may find ourselves wanting to internalize and isolate, edging out those closest to us and who understand us best—the people who could be key players in this introspective and spiritual point in our life. Feeling alone, the desires for these outlets, experiences, and connections increase the thirst for emancipation to become who we really want to be. Feelings of resentment over being misunderstood can infiltrate our most sober thinking.

In feeling alone, we often narrow what we see to our immediate circumference of influence and how things affect us personally at the time. We can feel that we have no one to turn to or talk with. It becomes hard to decipher mental noise from rational thought, and get to the information and stability that is best for all involved. We need to feel connected and to have a sense of purpose, and it helps to feel understood.

Drugs, alcohol, infidelity, financial squandering, family separations and divorce are all prevalent repercussions of personal changes that are improperly expressed and discussed. If the self-fulfilling prophecy of what we desire turns into what we fear most, it is because communication and aloneness sets in, and understanding shuts down. It is hard to find the peace we seek when we continue activities that can devastate our personal space, homes, and relationships. Choose your outlet wisely!

I often preferred being alone, and could sort it out or come around and stabilize to the approval of those around me—for the most part. If not, I would move on to a better space. As I said, I never really felt lonely. Eventually though, I turned to behaviors that were counterproductive and while alone, I also found myself deep in the throes of addiction. At first, I was relieving physical pain, and then emotional, then my disease turned on me and turned my life upside down. I was lonely, and then I felt alone, and then became addicted. Alone kept me from feeling understood, and a past history of judgment caused me to isolate further, until I eventually felt alone and away from God. Alone became dark. Alone became deadly!

Over time, an intervention and personal surrender placed me alone in a care facility for a handful of weeks. I found being honest, open, and willing was paramount to never feeling alone again. I haven't felt alone since. I have seen alone and what it can do. Alone has taken the lives of a few friends, the dignity of many others, and frequently kept me disconnected from people and that which I desired for many years.

Many people share these feelings and simply wish to communicate what is stirring within them without being judged. If you ever feel that you have a thought or interest that is exclusive to yourself or even odd, and find that you are starting to feel alone, take a lap through your neighborhood bookstore. You can also go online, or join a club. There are publications and groups that are extraordinarily unique, and are looking for members. I mean, you could probably find a blog or support group for vegetarian cowboy pagan basket weavers if you looked hard enough.

I have made the decision to not feel wrong or strange any longer. It is okay to experience boredom and feel wanting from time to time. Internalizing is not the answer. Try to communicate and start a search for what will nourish you. A hobby can soothe a restless mind. Seeking fellowship through religious or social groups; or spiritual growth through reading, meditation, study, and writing are helpful. Perhaps try a combination of all the above. All these can be integrated carefully and discreetly into your current lifestyle to help you feel more vibrant; that your life is vivid, has meaning, and remains fulfilling.

By communicating and connecting to new sources, we can see that we are not alone, and are more often in a majority. Being honest, open, and willing about our needs, and seeking like-minded people or those trained to help is essential.

If reading this finds you in a crisis, and you feel alone, start a dialogue about your feelings with someone you trust, a person who will not impose judgment on you. Research your dreams. Find something to listen to or read that interests you and that is uplifting and inspiring. Find an activity that provides you with a physical avenue to express yourself. Meditate or simply find a few moments of quiet time each day. Contemplate what is important to you, what you desire, and what you believe in. Finally, come to terms that it is okay to be you, and if you study and practice what makes you a better you, it will be easier to find the peace you seek and deserve, as well as the space and comfort to enjoy it. All this is so much easier and less expensive than a divorce or a sports car!

I now look at being alone as a time to regroup. To me it is like when I clean out my closet. I don't invite others to join me. I quietly empty the hold, decide what is a keeper, what needs to go, and then I reorganize. The task makes my closet able to hold more and newer things, and it is better organized and less chaotic. I also get the satisfaction of tending to a task that is often neglected, becomes long overdue, and makes room in my life. There is less clutter, life gets streamlined, and I become more receptive to the next phase of what comes my way.

I also realize that when I need to dispel the darker side of feeling alone, I should not internalize and suffer in silence. This was often counterproductive as the introspection would turn me to feeling like a victim as opposed to experiencing a nurturing period of time. I lost sight of the lifeguard and the shore as I drifted, increasing my chances of drowning in despair. It is when I reach out I find a hand that reaches back. It is when I share, I find others who share. It is when I become open, others come in. I implore upon those who feel alone or lonely to reach out, seek a common connection, and participate, even if it feels foreign. I have found some of the greatest loves, friendships, and mentors—people who saved my life—when I stopped trying to navigate the waters alone.

Reflections

Do I feel alone or lonely at times?

Are these the same feelings or different to me?

Do I find these feelings energizing or draining?

Is it easy for me to reach out to others when I feel lonely or alone?

What makes me feel alone? Does it come from others or within me?

Do I stay in this state long, or can I pull out of it quickly?

Could I attend a support group, perhaps read or start a hobby to help me reconnect with myself and to improve my state?

What fills the void when I feel alone?

Fragments

Our past deeds do not need to become our current identity.

The peace I have after going through this experience is very powerful to me. This is an examination of the paths we take in life and the pondering of our values, as well as our position of receiving validation in the eyes of others—our apparent "worth" if you will. In short, what makes us special?

I have encountered times when I felt unworthy of grace, mercy, and even love. Perhaps it stemmed from a feeling of inadequacy based on past misdeeds; or from a feeling of having no valuable contribution to this world because I was "broken".

There was much symbolism and truth that was brilliantly and divinely revealed to me on the day I describe here. I am grateful for it. This not only opened my eyes to the message, but to many things. I found many of our deepest insights and other precious gifts are sometimes found in the most obscure, unique, and unexpected places.

One of my closest friends and his family had the fortune of being offered the use of a wonderful beach home on the coast of North Carolina over the Fourth of July holiday. My family was invited to spend the week with them at this luxurious slice of paradise.

The house sits less than a hundred yards from the Atlantic Ocean. The flanking view to the right was a wooden pier jutting its lengths outward into the watery depths perfect for a romantic walk. Directly out the back door is a postcard view of blue skies with white wisps of clouds. The blue-green variations of the water with white peaks of waves appeared and disappeared into the horizon where water and sky meet.

The air was pleasant and warm. The breeze was just enough to cool where the sun warms, and was strong enough to cause continual flapping of the fabric of my clothing. I really like it when my shirt catches the breeze like a sail, and I could hear it rush past my ears as I walked. If I wanted to hear sounds clearer, I must turn my head to mute the roar of the rushing wind. The waves lapped at the shoreline in a tempo with a sound that makes me think that the Earth is actually breathing. The sound was rhythmic and divine. It was a perfect setting and the perfect excuse for a walk this day.

Prior to my departure, I had a friend mention that she heard the sea was like an enormous "liquid energy crystal". After the extensive drive, and the days leading up to the trip, I could use the recharge of energy. My goal was to be able to at least just stand in the water, ankle deep, and just to look out over the water's majesty. I wanted to breathe with the ocean, and drink in the sea air.

The short stroll from the bridge connecting the house to the sand quickly reminded me why humans invented shoes. The sand was hot, and the vegetation hearty. It was not accommodating to the tender feet of a Midwesterner who wears shoes most of the year. I made it through the escalating heat of the sand, through the debris that had washed ashore. Eventually I made it to the layer of new shells and particles of sea matter that the tide was depositing in an irregular pattern on the sand. It reminded me of a heartbeat pattern displayed on an EKG report, but with smoother peaks and valleys. I decided to walk in the space where my footprints are seen only briefly before being recaptured by the water, but not too far into the ocean where the sand under my feet gets pulled by the tide out from under me. I like the yielding firmness of the moist sand with my feet being randomly baptized by a dousing of sea foam and waves.

The sand was full of shells and shell fragments. Upon closer inspection, the sand was composed of what appeared to be ground up shells as opposed to the grains I was more familiar with. The beach had a mosaic path of small shells extending as far as the eye could see. It was about six feet wide and stretched the length of the beach as far as my eye could trace it, and had millions of shells strewn about. Many of the shells were the familiar flat scallop variety, and others appeared to be oyster shells. Most though, were small, and approximately the size of coins. The largest ones were about the size of a child's fist. They were surrounded in a menagerie of broken shells that never reached souvenir store quality, and would never see the shelves or displays, let alone a price sticker. Most of the mixture of shells and sea shrapnel was dominated by unrecognizable shards, as opposed to the intact wonders from my childhood memories.

Since the pieces posed a challenge to my tender bare feet, I walked just alongside the mixture closest to the water. I headed down the beach toward the pier for a moment of private reflection and solitude. I figured if I were lucky, I may find a piece of lost treasure! I didn't plan on being able to quit my day job, but a few pretty shells for my desk as a memento did seem possible. I only took one or two paces before I stooped to grab a couple of scallop shells. Rinsing the clinging sand in the surf, I inspected them and continued looking for a few more to add to my pockets. Most that I grabbed those first few steps were common and typical. They were the flat kind, fanning ridges radiating outward like the sun's rays with the little nose on top.

Soon, I noticed others objects glistening, like amber-colored stained glass. They were thin and reflective, and caught my eye. They appeared to be fragments rather than complete shells, but they were interesting, shiny, and beautiful. They stood out among the others even if they were imperfect. The ones I initially grabbed got cast back into the sea from where they originated, as I noticed something drawing me now to these newer treasures. The amber shell pieces ranged mainly in size to that of a quarter, to a contact lens, and they were equally as fragile. I traced the ridges with my fingers, and admired the polish the ocean placed upon them. I put the slivers in my front shirt pocket and proceeded down the beach. I was not searching, just observing the sandy path and Mother Nature's art before me.

As I plodded along in a lazy pace, I noticed that my gaze was continually drawn to the ground in front of me. I appreciated the pieces and patterns that moments ago were simply "litter" on the beach. Although millions and millions of shells and fragments were continually being placed and replaced by the ocean, submitted for my approval, I noticed certain ones called out for my inspection and approval. I also realized that the pieces that were calling to me were indeed just that—pieces! My eye kept going to the irregular shapes with brilliant colors and unfamiliar textures. These pieces were worn smooth in many instances. The others were adorned with Swiss cheese-like holes, becoming artifacts of the perfect museum. The tossing and tumbling, as well as torment and turbulence of the sea, sculpted these pieces into tiny gems. Broken and brilliant, they evolved from just one of a million, to one in a million. Their life, their battle, their journey, and their story gave them a noticeable uniqueness that set them apart from the others. They no longer were "typical" or "just another," they had become extraordinary through the weather and wear they endured.

Oddly, as my collection grew, I noticed that even among the millions of shells and pieces, something gave these objects their character. Perhaps it was their diminutive size. What I had noticed is that the shells with the intact forms, the "perfect" ones from my youth, had duller colors, sharper surfaces, and blended in with those around them. I bet if I collected a hundred, they would be similar in size, quality, and shape. What made my current collection special to me was the beautiful patterns the fragments had underneath that were exposed through the extreme ongoing wear they endured. The ocean's punishment made them smooth and pleasing to the touch. Their journey made them rich with interest, and they were engaging to be in the presence of. It was their past damage that gave them their current glow!

This was one of those times when I received a deep sense of gratitude. I got what I believed God was telling me. I have encountered many wise people, and I find that much of their, as well as my, newfound wisdom comes not from our achievements, but from the obstacles and hurdles we have passed through. Unfortunately, too many people believe the misdeeds of their past label them: "not worthy" or "beyond salvation" or "unable to receive enlightenment." (I have myself felt that I was, or deserved to be, forsaken as many of my thoughts or deeds would never allow me to be in the presence of grace, or permit me to connect with the Divine.) I have heard: "I'm not worth saving." "What I've done is too horrible." "God must hate me!" These and many other statements of why people are spiritually doomed are often common expressions we may hear.

I believe it is our pain that allows us to value our healing process. As with any infirmity or sickness, it takes time to rebound, but we must seek that which removes the illness and insures proper recovery. We must respect what caused us our unfortunate circumstances, but that respect accompanies knowledge that we can share and shine upon others to possibly shorten their duration in life's forge. It is by seeing our past travels as a path to enlightenment. By connecting and sharing with the willingness to serve others, either to intercept the negative patterns, or to be there after a tumble, is what allows us to gain spiritual momentum. It is our past obstacles that smooth our edges and bring out the underlying brilliance. It will only make our story richer. It is not my story that makes me less worthy, but more capable of seeing the path to becoming more awake. It is by sharing and helping others, and by bestowing my weathered fragments to them that embellishes my internal peace and self-worth.

I finally realize that when I felt forsaken, alone, unworthy, and unable to be forgiven, I was in the midst of something special, and something divinely guided. Like those shell fragments, I was being tossed and tumbled for a reason. My story gives me interest and character. It allows me insight to better serve others along my way. My edges are being smoothed, and my inner colors released for the world to see. It is through the adversity that is placed by God's hand before me that my life will receive its true luster.

I have a jar full of these fragments on my desk to remind me daily of my walks on that beach and the message I received. I have even made a couple of necklaces out of them to keep them even closer to me. I now look at my obstacles differently. Instead of seeing things from the bottom of the valley, I see the beginning of a mountainous ascent, with the gift of experience and knowledge waiting for me at the summit. It is a gift I can share with others to serve them by hopefully shortening the duration of their strife in a similar situation.

We can diminish our suffering by reducing that of others. When we emerge victorious, and when we are able to overcome obstacles or crises, we then have the ability to connect with others in a unique way. It is through our pain that we gain strength! I see that where I have once conquered, I can once again. Redemption is found in sharing with others to spare their suffering. It truly is our turbulence that polishes us to where we can reflect light not only on ourselves, but to brighten the path of others.

Reflections

Do I have difficulty sharing issues about my past? Do I feel guilty or shameful about it?

Do I feel detached, unworthy, or beyond redemption and forgiveness?

Do I see where sharing my experiences could prevent others from venturing down a similar path, alleviating some of their suffering?

Do I feel stronger or weaker from my experiences?

Have I ever considered using my experiences to help others through theirs?

Can I reach out to them now?

Can I see the possibility of how I can gain from my past sufferings?

Do I feel people think more or less of me because of what I have endured?

Something Greater

I find it more disturbing than comforting in the bold thinking that we are alone, and this is all there is.

I honestly did not feel I needed anyone or anything in my life. I considered my ability to fly solo a sign of strength or something to be admired. Of course I liked people, I loved others, but since I was comfortable with myself, I felt if others were in my life, it was a bonus, but still not a necessity. I felt this mostly in the context of having or needing a Higher Power, or the presence of a relationship with God or my Creator. I was a fair-weather religious practitioner—key word being "fair"—and went to church to make an appearance. I was not opposed to or against religion or God, but the actual necessity to appear in a building at a certain time to be considered faithful or a believer always puzzled me.

I often called out to God when I needed something, either of the material nature or for alleviation of pain or suffering. I rarely offered thank you's when my prayers were answered, or when I noticed I was in receipt of any form of blessing. Selfishly, I did not see the tangible return on investment. I often looked to God as a child does to Santa Claus. For example, I would ask for a specific toy, then on Christmas morning would knock my folks out of the way to get to the tree and open many, many wonderful packages that were given to me. When not finding the one thing I specifically asked for, I would pout and question the validity of my beliefs in him. I would often find it difficult to muster the ability to enjoy the multitude of other gifts I received, let alone even thank Santa. I often treated my spirituality in this manner. I see now that I am, and always have been, blessed with abundance, and appreciate the joys of this moment and a true connection with whom my gifts originate.

I have always subscribed to the belief that there was something and or some "one" responsible for hosting this show we call life. For many years, I did not feel that I needed any sort of regular contact with this entity, but carried an awareness and respect that we are merely players, and we should "be good" and do the best we can. We should leave the rest to fate, and if we were dutiful and wanted a bit of inside help, we could go to a church, synagogue, temple, or group, to help us find what we were looking for. If we attended, fine; but if not, depending on whom you talked to, you were doomed, your fate was already planned, or it didn't matter. Either mindset left me feeling a lot of what we experienced in our human form up was to us, as well as what we physically did or practiced to get the most out of life. We just may get punished for some of our actions, or rewarded for good behavior.

I was raised by hardworking parents whose efforts put clothes on our back, food on the table, and a roof over our heads. We lived "good", were "good" people, "good" things happened for us, and so life remained "good", if we continued to be "good". We were holiday church goers, and when attending, we did as the others did: we sang the hymns, prayed the prayers, and knelt when told following the groups direction. When the hour or so was up, we would adjourn to the fellowship hall for coffee and doughnuts and some idle banter assuming blindly that our spiritual batteries were now recharged. When not attending, I still noticed the same highs and lows, and the same life circumstances, and could still socially mingle with my church going brethren through the week, so prayer, Higher Powers, and mandated attendance dropped in priority as I assumed all is "good", as it should be. I went on with my life sans any weekly spiritual or religious fellowship or study. This went on for most of my teen and adult life. I was not at all opposed to those who found joy in it. I just found I was more surrounded by people who practiced and professed that it was more of a world that embraced and acknowledged the mindset of education, ambition, networking and partying, and getting things done was how we elevated ourselves.

In my adulthood, I observed that people saw education and career as tantamount in getting ahead and achieving success, as well as the ability to retire, be happy, provide, and become fulfilled. It was of extreme importance to learn as much as I could, surround myself with successful self-made people, and learn their secrets of success. Then happiness and fulfillment would surely be mine.

Anyone who has ever watched late night TV can see a couple of things. Primarily, there are those who believe that something greater is out there, **and** for three simple and easy payments of some dollar amount and ninety five cents, (plus shipping and handling,) you too could have your problems solved, and life will then improve for you. You can become: thinner, have better things, quit your day job, and have the opposite sex find you more attractive, have a larger bank account, be more at peace, and even have healthier bowel movements!

The other thing I noticed is that some man or woman has the proven secret or system, and that it is only a phone call or website away. They will be your guru, and are willing to share this wealth of knowledge for a fee. But wait! If you hurry right now, you can receive their newsletter absolutely free! It can't get any better than that! No faith, no work involved, no prayer, no nothing, but a mere credit card, check or money order! You too, can have everything you ever need or want, and your problems solved, so pick up the phone now! Better yet, if it doesn't work, you can send it back for a full refund (minus the shipping and handling). Why bother with fifty-two Sundays or Saturdays of reading, prayer, devotion, fellowship or spiritual practice and study? Why bother with spiritual practices?

Being a public speaker, I would try to find tips and tricks that worked for me, and share them through a microphone, or sometimes in an occasional workshop, or magazine article. If people would follow these points, they too could have success, skill or whatever other coveted item I offered. I also sought out mentors and speakers, studied their skills, and added them to my repertoire. This way I could cut out the middleman of having to find my own path and simply use the other guy's map. I always believed there was "Something Greater" than myself. I would shoot out a few token prayers here and there, respected that it was His show, but felt that someday I could become happy, and have what the other blessed people enjoyed. I knew it was somewhere here on Earth, I had just not found it yet. I kept searching from book to book, tape to tape, speaker to speaker, city to city, person to person, feeling close at times, but it was like I was chasing a rainbow. It moved as I approached.

As my life proceeded, and I entered my late thirties and early forties, I noticed my highs were higher and my lows became lower. I had lost my ability to stabilize. I was at the mercy of the circumstances in which I found myself. If things were going well, I might look to the heavens and give a wink or a nod, perhaps an attaboy, but that was about it. If things were bad, I felt I was forsaken and lost with no way of getting home. There seemed to be no intention for my life, no plan, no alignment. I eventually started to feel there was nothing greater out there, and my life seemed to be a series of comedic and cosmic accidents.

It took a series of these circumstances to make me realize it was time to tune-in to a new channel. I needed to look to a new source for my interests, and to cultivate a new direction for my personal growth. These circumstances brought me to a place of surrender.

Now surrender was not something I was going to do easily. It was not desirable at all. No man wants to feel defeated, over-powered, or like he must throw down his gun and start the march of shame. But this time surrender meant, "You tried, you gave it your best; let someone or something more qualified have a turn at the wheel." So, unlike becoming a P.O.W., I felt like I had hopped in the passenger seat, and was letting someone who knew how to get where we were going take us home. After figuratively driving around a strange, scary neighborhood for a long time, someone who knew how to get home was at the wheel. I was tired. I was lost. I was humbled. I decided to have faith outside my own ego for a change. I decided to seek, embrace, practice, and connect with a Higher Power, with Something Greater!

What I found most beneficial to me is the realization that my connection to the Divine is truly a relationship. That means there is an ongoing give and receive of salvation and service, as well as therapeutic dialogue and communication channels that must be kept open to insure growth. I also had to find and attach myself to the value of the relationship for me to desire to stay connected. I had to continue to seek improvement, and to practice the necessary spiritual restoration when things got off alignment. I needed to observe and validate why I needed this particular union. It came down to a few simple but important characteristics. I had all I needed to bring to the table, and in turn I could receive the blessings I so desperately sought for years.

The first was love. I could love God as a parent who gave me life, and not have to wait for an "I love you, too," or a card, flowers, or a parental pat on the head. I would not be disappointed, laughed at, cheated on, or shamed. Like a good parent, I can feel secure that when my actions need attention, or improvement or direction, I am still loved, and my best interests are held in high regard. It is with that love I can love myself. If I am good enough for God, I can surely love me, and perhaps others can too. If I have a good relationship with myself,

I am more likely to have quality interactions with those around me. Like a child who feels and knows love, my true nature can shine, because I know someone or something always has my back! Love of this nature fortifies my faith, as I just have to love. With God, I love; therefore it is. I have faith I am loved, therefore I am.

Second, I seek and receive improved life navigation. I seek what I believe is right and true in my thought, word, and deed. Like a child who acts, and then looks to see if the parent is watching, I find myself acting similarly. I look outside myself for the benefit of my actions and how I may serve. You are probably familiar with these mantras: "What would Jesus do?" and "I want to think like God thinks." They direct me away from my ego, and direct me toward that of a greater purpose, and of better service to others. I believe God is the magnetic force that keeps my needle aimed in the right direction. It is through prayer, meditation, and processing, that I stay on the correct path and outside of myself to stay aware and in tune with my greater life's purpose. God helps me adjust my rudder as I navigate life's currents. I find peace in this relationship. I find that there is Divine reason, purpose, intention, and direction for me. I find it hard to not think that Something is in charge, Something created it, and to think all this is an accident is just not as calming for me personally.

Finally, I like the fact that with God, we cannot complain to, or confront Him as we can with a spouse, boss, or political figure when something does not go our way. We must be humble, have faith, and let go of our egos and be patient. I look at results differently. They are not an end but rather part of an ongoing life drama. Since I cannot whine or complain upon tangible ears, I have to reflect and connect to my inner core and my faith, and wait for an answer. Right now, the answer might simply be "no."

I now realize I have God's love, navigation, and peace available to me. Knowing there is Someone Greater to celebrate with, and to help me make sense of the senseless is calming.

My Higher Power, Source, or Creator, may not be the same as yours. However, I hope that whatever or whomever you find as your source of love and inspiration gives you solace and peace. May your connection become your beacon in the storm. May you find a new avenue of unconditional love. If you find that somehow you may have ended up in the ditch, it is nice to let someone else take the wheel.

I know for some people this subject is a tough pill to swallow. It was for me. It is hard to place unconditional faith in something you cannot grasp in your hands. I try to feel divinity in my heart as opposed to my fingers. I often judged God's credibility by my own selfish interpretations. I asked for divine presence and manifestation of grace in my own egotistical definitions. I wanted what I wanted, when I wanted it, and if there was no answer, there was no God!

My beliefs and trust allow me to connect without judgment now, and my connection to the Divine is the glue that binds me to others, my purpose, and myself. It gives me peace to know I coincide with the intention placed before me. It feels to me like when I tell my kids, "Daddy loves you," and they smile contently with the satisfied look of knowing the truth behind the statement. They simply **know** that the feeling is mutual. I now display that contented smile.

I invest rather than demand. I practice patience, and I try to develop my awareness of God's presence in my life as opposed to where He isn't. I hope you find your way home to Something Greater, and that it truly feels like home.

Reflections

Do I have trouble believing in Something Greater than myself?

What are the hurdles and obstacles I see in trying to develop this connection?

Can I see the potential benefits and positives?

Do I believe there is only one belief system, or do I think it is more of a personal interpretation or relationship?

Do I feel I need more inspiration or education to achieve this kind of connection?

Do people who express faith in Something Greater intimidate me? Why?

Am I willing to reach out and research avenues that best fit my needs and lifestyle?

Can I start a dialogue with others in matters of spiritual connection?

Cut!

The harder I fall, the higher I can bounce!

*At times I have felt that our lives play out like theatrical productions. In movies, as well as our lives, it seems the more conflict present, the more riveted we become. Conflict is inevitable. It is how we **deal** with conflict that allows it to emerge in our lives as a teacher or torturer. It is funny how we always seem to wish life would pick up the pace, but once the excitement starts, we desire to go back to the way things used to be when they were nice and quiet.*

We can become the "directors" of our lives, and we can also create and dictate the tone, pace, and duration of the "scenes." If we are wise, we can artistically manage the scenes to a greater degree than we currently try to. We can embrace the organic and spontaneous occurrences that enrich the movie-going experience, for all watching.

I view my personal quest as one of trying to achieve serenity and balance, merged with peace, happiness, and fulfillment. My journey was often interrupted by conflicts that made it hard for me to stay true to my chosen direction. These random circumstances were hurdles I had to overcome to once again get back in the happy lane. "Happy" is such a relative term, but I would say my definition is: "No presence of great conflict, and a lack of major obstacles in my journey. It is to be able to travel my path unmolested so nothing can easily disturb my serenity. It is also to maintain appreciation of that which occurs within and around me." These properties can exist inclusive or exclusive of each other, and most of the time is controlled by my personal perceptions.

Conflict would occasionally appear and stand in the way of my happiness or satisfaction, and until conquered, peace and progress were impeded. I am not talking about simple instances such as a stain on a shirt, alarm clock not going off, relationship spats, or lost car keys, but rather events that are more impacting and more difficult to get over. The times when I wanted to yell, "Cut!" through a director's megaphone.

I have experienced parental divorce, health issues, lost loves, unmet goals, financial challenges, addiction, family estrangement, career problems, marital conflicts, and many things that didn't go my way. Each one affected me like Kryptonite, draining my strength and soul.

To me, life is similar to a movie. There is the character's introduction and the establishment of their role. There is a plot element, a conflict, often a twist, and then there is a point when the actors encounter one another, and interact in the situation. The plot element then embeds itself in the storyline, creates conflict, or is overcome. Our lives are simply a long line of sequels connected without intermissions.

We, in a sense, are like a director/actor. We star in our own movie, as well as get behind the camera to help direct. However in life's script, we have a tendency to challenge or get angry with the changes, thinking only what is perceived, or currently established in our "script" is acceptable. The reality is: life doesn't follow a script. If we are to have a lead role in our movie, we must come to terms with this fact.

Conflict for me is exacerbated by a few simple components. The first component is my often unrealistic expectations. I expected one thing, another happened. Boom! Conflict! Expectations are when we go beyond the truth of what truly is, and decide to write our own script based on how we think things should happen, how they should feel, should act, and should think. Should being a key word here! (I have heard if you should all over people, they will should all over you too!) We displace our actions, desires, and beliefs, and impose them on others, implying our parameters should become theirs.

The next element is control. We don't like when our expectations are not met, but even more so when things go beyond our ability to control them. We try to control people, nature, time, emotions, health, aging, and a multitude of things beyond our true ability. I prefer to try to manage things. I try to look at circumstances with an eye that seeks flexibility to be able to adapt to the best of my personal skill.

Control often makes us look for the fault or point of departure from the norm. We then focus our energies on dominating and restabilizing the person or occurrence until it fits our script. My father used to say "it is like putting puppies in a box." For example, you put one in, one jumps out. You grab that one, and two others are now fighting. You stop those two, and find one peeing in the corner, and on and on. Controlling the situation is futile. We must learn to navigate life as opposed trying to control and direct it. Learn to love your puppies.

Labels are another element when dealing with conflicts. How we choose to look at something determines not only our perception, but also the duration and the outcome. It truly affects what gets manifested before us! We can deviate from the truth of a situation and embellish it with a label of our choosing. Labels leverage how we feel about something, and therefore place ourselves in a victim or aggressor position rather than observing something for what it simply is.

For example:

> **Truth:** "He and I have grown apart and should explore a better life for ourselves separately."
>
> **Label:** "She/he just doesn't get me, so we are divorcing which is ruining my life and everything else!"
>
> **Truth:** "I do not feel fulfilled in my job and it is time for me to seek other options to give me more satisfaction."
>
> **Label:** "This place sucks and the boss is keeping me from being all I could be!"
>
> **Truth:** "I have fifty-seven cents in the bank."
>
> **Label:** "I am broke and a loser!"

If we stay aware and focus on the truth of a situation, we can see that it simply is what it is. It is not a personal attack on us. We can then step back and see what we can do to achieve a positive resolution rather than focus on seeking retribution, passing judgment, or applying labels that cause pain and create further suffering. Labels become not just words, but also belief systems and prejudices. They can reappear in the future without warning. They can even go beyond being used in one situation to a more global labeling pattern. This can transcend from being used once, to a blanketing and perpetual belief such as when someone says: "A*ll* men are childish" or "A*ll* women are cheaters.

We can always step back and ask ourselves what are we to learn from an experience, so potentially every conflict can pay a beneficial dividend. Of course, no one welcomes challenging circumstances and pain. On the other hand, it can lead to an appreciation of our normalness, which can be lost if not occasionally punctuated from time to time with script changes.

I just pray that the movie called "my life" is more comedy/drama as opposed to tragedy. In this epic in which we all star in, (as well as co-direct), we have to remember that we do not have the chair with our name on the back or the bullhorn, and when we do not like what we see, we cannot yell "Cut!"

I now try to focus on my character development and the eventual message that is going to be revealed. Conflict is often stretched ad nauseum by our inability to accept things as they are, and the expectations we impose on others and the world around us. When we try to direct or control the uncontrollable, we often increase the intensity and duration of a situation by inflating its challenge and menacing presence. This is often in direct proportion to the level we perceive the resolution is out of reach.

Reflections

Is it difficult for me to accept things as they are?

Do I often wonder why the rest of the world doesn't see things the same way I do?

Do I enter into relationships and situations with expectations in place beforehand?

Have these expectations created or presented conflicts for me?

Are the expectations I place on myself and others realistic?

Could I live under the parameters of the expectations I place on others?

Do I accept others the way I wish to be accepted?

When discussing my conflicts with others, do they see things the same way I do, or am I accused of making too much out of things, or of taking things too lightly?

Bookends

I refuse to judge my life by one event any more than I would judge an entire song by one note!

It is in the bookends framing an event where acceptance, understanding, and learning dwell. If we look at specific events in small finite chunks, we lose the eternal cosmic value that the actual event can inspire. It is when we cease our desire to frame things in the judgmental perspective of individual chapters, and see them as part of a never-ending story; we can have peace that a resolution is coming, and that the truth will eventually be revealed for our greater good!

What has been exciting for me as I pursue a new level of meaning in my life and a healthier perspective is that at the time and place when I most need it, people and solutions have magically seemed to appear. Some of these people are from deep in the archives of my life, some have been with me all along, and others are newfound friends and acquaintances. The most interesting thing, though, is how perfectly they fit into my life where they enter or reappear. They often enter with the right message, the right talent, or needed wisdom or support.

One of these people is a long-lost friend who I recently reconnected with via an Internet social networking site. We have shared the "whatever happened to so-and-so" volleys, as well as have caught up on our kids, jobs, and roads traveled. It has been fun finding we have similar histories, dreams, and mindsets now. Twenty-five years ago we discussed spirituality, humanity, and the mystical and it is interesting to compare where we are today from where we stood back then. The past and the present are fluid elements that bookend a story that falls in between, which brings us to where we are now.

My new old friend invited me to a fireside chat at a mutual friend's home in a small quaint town not far from where I live. I was promised an eclectic group of like-minded people from a variety of backgrounds discussing topics of a spiritual nature. The setting was inviting, the people friendly, and the attendance of old friends an added bonus. Excited, I drove the hour to attend.

The hostess had the setting dressed beautifully with a welcoming fire pit, a lush green glen offering harbor for friends enjoying food, fellowship, and light banter. The cross-section had people young and old, male and female, varying sexual orientations, religious practices, spiritual beliefs, as well as the academic and untrained in matters of the mystical. Each person brought a distinct flavor and contribution, regardless of whether they chose silence or to dominate the floor with their thoughts.

The discussions varied from people addressing the entire circle, to those engaging the person nearby. The structure's looseness was what made it engaging and not threatening. I felt safe in whatever words I chose to offer.

We discussed many topics, some deeper than others, and we were blessed by two of the group members to have musical talents. They happened to bring their instruments with them for ambient serenade. The sun was setting, the music serene, the fire was warm, and our hearts were content.

After a while with a few light discussions under our belt, we entered into a topic I will call "Divine intervention." This is my term and may not be shared by the others, but it is simply to set up where I am going. We were discussing if every event in history, whether perceived now as good or bad, as well as all of humanity itself, were placed in their respective places in time for the greater good. We also discussed if they were from a Divine source. In short, we wanted to see how everyone felt about the notion that all events are from God, Source, or Creator, and if they are a "blessing" no matter how they were delivered or received.

A discussion ensued as people challenged how one could receive a lesson, goodness, or a blessing from horrific situations, disasters, and holocausts. "How can this have any good?" "Where is the divine presence in it", were some of the challenging questions.

The reference of Hitler's reign and the murderous annihilation of the Jews were raised as an example. How could this event, one of the lowest in the history of man, show any light or good? How can tsunamis and other natural disasters, genocide, global warming, racial and religious persecution in any way be Divine and thought of as an eventual blessing? As the discussion flowed, I reflected back to events I had endured personally in my life path, (addiction, cancer, death, estrangement, relationship challenges, and financial hardship) and had a hard time seeing any blessing let alone anything resembling a "gift from God".

My epiphany came to me around the fire that night. I call it my awareness of **spatial perspective**. I believe that all of this, the past, now, and time beyond, started at a point and then began expanding. Call it the Big Bang, divine creation, or whatever you believe to be the actual beginning. It doesn't really matter here (to abstain from a distracting debate) as to when that was. From there, the interaction and expansion of things had a "source or divine intention." Through the expansion, beings, circumstances, and a multitude of events combined and connected to continually intertwine and create more and more of these ongoing and ever-changing events. All these interactions and circumstances blend harmoniously and lead into a dynamic that causes things to occur and change and evolve, continually expanding outward and onward infinitely.

Only one thing is certain: nothing stays the same forever. In looking at a chunk of time, if we "bookend" it and leave out the events leading up to and eventually resulting from it, we observe only one part of the story and place a label on it based on our current perspective. We can say that any of the aforementioned events are "bad" because of how narrowly we place the bookends, and how we exclusively focus in between them and look at the event itself from a biased perspective. If the bookends are narrowed to only give focus on the event itself. Then if it is personalized, and then if we place now as the ending, the "game over," if you will. It is easy to see how a situation can be deemed more tragic or insurmountable. (Although the examples I mentioned are very unpleasant, I hope you will bear with me.)

What I saw, and tried to share with my friend was this: First, let's move the first bookend of our spatial perspective to the beginning, I mean way back, as far as we can. Since it is not my time, but everyone's time, we cannot lay claim to when this event truly started or began, so let's not focus on a definite "when it all began" as our existence was set in motion long before our presence on Earth. Secondly, we do not know when humanity's days will end, let alone our own personal end for that matter. We should not place a finality on our now; meaning we must realize and find peace in the fact that the "story ain't over yet!" We can look at our current difficulties as simply stoplights on our way home.

How often have we been in situations that at the time seemed hopeless, devastating, crippling or terminal, and eventually over time we, and others, have emerged stronger and wiser? How often have we seen this happen to those around us or in the news? We hear people speak of becoming thankful over time for their struggles. If not always right here, or right now, we can see testimony to the fact that these blessings and miracles do indeed happen. The gifts and blessings in everything are revealed in the time frame that is most beneficial to those destined to receive them; no sooner no later. Time does not belong to us, nor can we control how it unfurls and what happens within.

In the cases of illnesses and addictions, these can prompt others to reexamine their health and behaviors to perhaps help them live better or even save their lives. Individual suffering can be a blessing by helping scores of others by sharing lessons learned. That is why in groups such as Alcoholics Anonymous, it is so important for people to share their stories with others. Not only for examples of what they overcame, and how far they fell, but to be an example of hope to the listeners.

In broader examples, such as the Holocaust, and natural and manmade disasters; these events propelled an action toward a global remedy. They spark an elevated awareness, and a movement to protect ourselves from this ever happening again. We have to try to examine things on a broader level, and to be patient for the message to be revealed, and indeed it always is revealed to the benefit of those needing it. It is always part of the intended plan and for the greater good of humanity; it is how the universe reconciles itself after certain transactions and how things become balanced. It sometimes may be the only comfort we can find in making sense of terrible circumstances.

Likewise, to appreciate love, we sometimes have to suffer a lack of love. To appreciate peace, sometimes war must present itself. Illness brings an appreciation of one's health.

Our perspective in time can alleviate a lot of our issues with a feeling of finality on certain subjects. It can help with our labels of whether something is truly good or bad in the grand scheme of life. When narrowing the bookends of our perspective, things can be monumentally reinforced as to how bad or how enduring they will be. We may feel that we alone suffer the burden exclusively. Expanding our scope and practicing patience can assure us to that which has been said many times: "this too shall pass." With patience and hindsight, our true gifts and lessons will be revealed to us. It is often through reflection and evaluation, and after we have crossed the chasm, which we are then allowed the awareness to the message contained in the event. Perhaps it is because we are then in a state of clarity and not chaos. We need to be in the proper place to receive the message for it to take root and endure.

As we closed our fireside chat that night, I felt more comfortable realizing my concept of spatial perspective can, if anything, allow me peace in knowing I am where I should be; at least for now and for the right reasons. Through the pain we will indeed grow and eventually move on. We will arrive where we are intended to land. Like that of a comprehensive and well-stocked bookcase, if we look at the volumes the bookends hold in between, we can see an abundance of knowledge there for reference, study, and entertainment. We can see that what is contained therein is not only for us, but to be shared with others.

Most importantly, we need to remember that bookends come in pairs. They are elastic and can accommodate fluctuations in the amount they contain. They are not bound from expanding when needed to welcome as much fresh wisdom as one wishes to place in between.

When I reflect back on that night, I remember it was a peaceful gathering of people simply trying to make sense of what seemed senseless and intolerable. I walked away with hope that what I and others may overcome smoothes the ground for others to tread upon. I know we do not always have the ability to make sense of certain situations, but we can make peace with them. We can decide that there is a Divine intention for everything going on, in and around us. If we are patient and have hope, the purpose, meaning, and blessings will eventually be revealed to us for the greater good of not only ourselves, but also for all mankind.

Reflections

Do I wrestle with seeing the positives in a challenging situation?

Do I view certain events as punishments, neutral, or blessings?

What helps me through tough times?

Do I view the circumstances in my life as separate events or as part of a never-ending story?

Can I look back and move my bookends to see where an event I considered bad or devastating actually was beneficial?

Can I do this for more than one event in my life?

How can I seek hope when challenges appear to be insurmountable and difficult?

Be Prepared

It is best to check your parachute for holes before you jump!

I am amazed by what I can achieve with duct tape, let alone by adding a hammer or a screwdriver. Our serenity and spirituality, like our dwellings, benefit from having a few useful tools at our disposal in case of a breakdown. We too need random maintenance and upkeep. If we spring a leak, the more accessible our tools, and the more tasks they are capable of tackling, the less down time we encounter, less residual damage, and the speedier we can get back to enjoying our peace of mind.

In this book, I share a few tricks of the trade I practice to help me stay where I want and need to be. Without some handy and simple ways to cope with, and recover from, a breakdown, we can find ourselves with growing issues and greater consequences. It is so much better to be prepared and tend to our stuff ahead of time.

There are many tools: meditation, yoga, sports, weight lifting, martial arts, walking, and singing, pet care, cooking, music, reading, writing, gardening, etc. The key is to having the tools that work for you, and having them handy, as the need for them can crop up unexpectedly. Examine what you have at your disposal in case you encounter an emotional leak or spiritual flat tire.

As the faint light of dawn peeked through the blinds, I noticed the bird's songs starting to come alive. The amber glow of the sunrise coming through the blinds that fell upon my slumbering and squinting eyes, told me it was much too early for me to rise. My alarm was set for the usual 7:00 A.M.., but I was sure it was at least an hour or two prior to its call. I didn't want to open my eyes, for fear my mind would start doing the math of how long I had until my morning routine would start. Most days my mind was willing to rise long before my physical self was ready.

My mind often starts to run through the day's itinerary with a noisy chatter: Rise, shower, wake the kids, etc. Is the coffee made? I hope so. Feed the dog. Don't forget your briefcase. What's the days' client list like? Is my wife gonna be in a pleasant mood? I think I hear her breathing. Leave her be. Gonna be an easy day or a hectic day? I dunno. It should be an easy day. Hope there's sun out today. I like sunny days. I don't mind rain that much either though. Don't forget to take your new CD in the car. On and on and on it goes. My mind takes off like a couch potato overdosed on energy drinks who is channel surfing. It takes a quick glance at the screen, listens for a second, then onto the next channel!

My mind is can be like a chatty little toddler just observing, questioning, yet with an attention deficit issue. "Dad, where are my shoes?" "I love you!" "What time is Spongebob on?" "Cereal is yummy." "I like fuzzy puppies." "Do you like puppies?" "Can we get a puppy?" "I have a blue bike." That gives you an idea of the randomness of my mind's hyper nature in comparing it to the questions of a child. (Maybe it is just my kids.)

I have heard that we have between 60,000 and 80,000 individual thoughts a day and most of them are repetitive. I have also heard the mind described as a "drunken baby monkey who just got stung by a scorpion!" I think we have all encountered this ability of our minds to just go on holiday at times. Like a child, it can test my patience, but if I respond with love and patience, and engage tolerance and peace, I can let it pass without disruption.

I used to spend a lot of time lying in bed talking myself off the ledge so-to-speak. I would emotionally dig deep to convince myself I could get through it all. Now I have the ability to detach and observe what is within me that needs attention. I can then become aware enough to realize that it is 5:00 A.M., and my creditors, kids, business, obligations, employees, as well as the rest of those things I typically deal with in my mind are probably still in bed sleeping. I can choose to join them. If X, Y, or Z is on my mind and it is important, it will probably be there later when I wake. If it is haunting me in bed, rest assured, it will pop up again on my mental or desktop calendar. I reassure myself that I am warm and comfortable, in bed, and then ask my mind to "turn off the noise" and to make a mental sticky note to remind me when I awaken for the day. It is also helpful to have actual sticky-notes at my bedside, just in case!

I then focus on my breathing, aware of the rhythm and peaceful unforced cadence each inhale and exhale makes. I visualize each breath like a wave crashing upon the sandy shore of a tropical beach. If I am truly awake, I engage my senses as completely as possible, still keeping up with the pace of the breath. This allows me to sink deeper into the relaxing picture I mentally paint.

It may be a hammock, swaying to and fro as I concentrate on the sunbeams finding their way through the dense palm fronds overhead. (It is all about the vividness of the picture.) I try to breathe with the increasing and decreasing of the summer Cicadas. I realize if I intercept the mental rantings, and can redirect the creative license my mind wants to take, and plug in some positive input and soothing direction. Eventually, I am able to drift off, or I may meditate until I am able to fall asleep again. At the least, I can maintain a state of relaxation until I choose to rise, which is a healthy precursor to my morning routines.

With my day's start gaining positive balance, I notice the small obstacles that can be placed in my way are just that: small obstacles. They are to be navigated around and not the damning, wrathful assassinations of my mental state as I once allowed them to be. Missing toothpaste lid? So. Is my favorite shirt in the laundry? Choose another. Out of creamer? Drink it black. All these situations have and will emerge, but how I choose to react is what has changed. Will I lose control? Absolutely! Can I be in a less than favorable disposition to my friends and family upon occasion? You betcha! I have heard it said before that "we are not human beings having a temporary spiritual experience, but spiritual beings having a temporary human experience" and that temporary human experience is where we can see our ego surface and can just let loose on some plain old bad behavior.

I now have the awareness of when I may derail and I give myself a well-needed timeout. I will try to do the homework of observing the disruption, get a plan together to manage it, and then try to overcome or move beyond it with any help I can muster and pray for.

I use a few tools to help my awareness. One happened by accident. I found myself "wowing" at my own actions from time to time. When I have a moment of disconnection or adverse behavior, or when I simply am being a grumpy brat, I will find myself noticing it, and then I respond with a "Wow!" It is involuntary and subconscious, but I am happy as it creates an awareness of my actions and thoughts, and bookmarks it for me to take an objective look at how I can get back on track. The "wow" is not that of a pleasant surprise, but that of a questionable concern for myself and allows me to look at the experience with a detached awareness as to how I can handle the situation better next time. It is like I say to myself, "Wow dude, settle down!" I am so thankful that I am able to at least catch it, even if a few seconds too late. At least then I can become accountable, and work on it.

I find deep breaths cleansing. I inhale and exhale slowly as I enter a new location, room, or situation. I fill my lungs and drink in the scents and aromas that trigger certain thoughts, states, and memories. With the multitude of fragrances, both good and bad, I try to lock onto a pleasant scent or sense that I encounter, and try to spend a second or two and just give it my entire focus. This allows me to hit the "reset" button and gain a clearer connection of where I am, and what I am doing. It can also take something apparently mundane, boring, familiar, or redundant, and give it new life. It allows me to be aware that "I am here" and "I am here, right now!" Not only is the cleansing nature of the oxygen beneficial, but the added sense of the olfactory stimulation is that much more of a connection for me.

I also use visual analysis. I scan my environment with more focus and try to pick out things I used to miss. I connect for a second. I don't allow judgment to enter into the analysis, but simple observation without any labeling or opinion if I can. I may notice a dominating texture, such as a great amount of hard or soft surfaces; or perhaps brilliant colors. In my yard there are many soothing shades of green. I pay attention to the varying colors and depth of the hues. I notice the minute and the grand, the detailed and the bland.

For example, this morning on my way to work, I noticed the way the morning sun's rays caused an interesting and animated mosaic of light and shadows that pierced the foliage and created interesting patterns on the landscape. I also remember the soothing "swoosh" of the passing cars from my fellow travelers heading in the opposite direction as I listened through my open car window. I remember the fog on the river, and the relative brightness of the sun on the water in between the fog banks. I remember the smell of my coffee in my mug pleasantly becoming stronger as I raised it to my mouth for a sip. I simply try to connect and become aware to what has always been there. Just in more vivid detail.

What used to frustrate me easily can provide me with insight and a lesson on growth. I can eventually derive joy from it all. What others may try to complain away or wish away, I try to yield to and become flexible in my approach. I try to gain elasticity to where I can gain more acceptance and meaning from many situations that used to cripple me into immobility. I used to think, like in martial arts, that with attendance, practice, and diligence I could eventually get a black belt and be strong enough to tackle whatever came my way. I am now called to reflect on a quote from Bruce Lee's *Tao of Jeet Kune Do* stating: "It is not daily increase, but daily decrease" that we must learn and practice. It is not just accumulation of knowledge and skill, but also letting go of that which is not beneficial to us which is the key. It is essential to be able to grasp what is new and useful, yet we have to also let go of certain things that may be taking up space and energy that occupies where something positive can reside. Our nature is we like to accumulate more than we care to let go of. The paradox I see, which brings me to the joy I feel, is that the more I get rid of, the more I have.

I realize my healthy perceptions are among the most valuable tools I have that can determine how my day goes. I practice humility and try to be aware when my ego infiltrates my space and starts its corruption. I read, pray, meditate, and listen with my head and my heart, looking for growth, peace, and connection at every possible encounter. I realize I am not alone and never have to be. Most importantly, I realize that one of the greatest and most rewarding ways to gain and to cultivate spiritual growth is in the service of your fellow man (and woman). There is no greater return on investment as in that of serving others, especially those in need. Having compassion and offering of me and my time is very beneficial to my well-being.

All these factors provide potential for a quantum shift in our life. We will stumble. We will backslide. There will be ups and downs and challenges along the way, which is to be expected. However, if we can love and forgive ourselves, our journey will appear less treacherous. We can obtain the tools to create a wonderful life for ourselves and the people around us. By using these simple tools, we can continually restore and renovate our soul—even when drama, destruction, and degradation confront us. It is progress and not perfection that we should seek. In turn, our life's valleys will be more shallow and our blessings much deeper!

My goal is to diffuse and neutralize that which appears to disarm or disrupt me. I use awareness, processing, acceptance, and forgiveness instead of anger, frustration, blame, and addiction. I activate the tools I have until I find the one that offers relief. Most importantly, I seek progress and not perfection in others and myself—which is key.

I never feel that all is perfect forever, or that I can rest on my laurels. I have to be aware that something can always spring a leak and will need repair. If I have a set of tools at my disposal that vary in their usefulness and that I am rehearsed in using, I can be more relaxed knowing I am prepared and have solutions—a "lifeguard on duty" if you will. Like in first aid, the best time to stock the kit and read the field manual is long before the bleeding starts.

Reflections

Do I have a variety of tools at the ready to help me tackle life's challenges?

Am I open to new techniques to relieve me from that which is harmful, and to heal me in the event of a challenge?

What hobbies bring me joy or peace?

Do I use simple exercises such as meditation, stretching, or breathing to bring me back to a peaceful or calm state when needed?

What activities or exercises, either alone or with others, can I use to regroup or help me maintain a healthy state?

Is it difficult for me to calm or center myself?

Can I stabilize myself without dwelling on what is bothering me and without turning to destructive outlets?

Final Thoughts

The evolution I am experiencing is eye opening. It is simple yet profound. I realize what is, simply is. Although we can't control what happens, we can control how we react and how deep we let things affect us. We do not always get what we want or when we want it. The mundane can be a profound instructor. The old can become new with new perspective. Life's lessons appear all around us, in abundance, every day. It is our choice to be open to seeing and hearing them.

It is our choice to be receptive to take a seat in the universal classroom of personal growth and self-cultivation. We do not need to feel ripe and beaten down, forsaken, or lost. We must simply practice being awake and aware to the fact that things as simple as taking a walk, time spent with loved ones, a smell in the air, shells on the beach, may be God's way of getting our attention, and that "church" is wherever, and whenever you find it.

We must remember that we need to do the work—with no homework comes no passing grade. The most wonderful thing about this, though, is this class has no tuition. The teachers are willing, abundant, and will not give up on us, and school does not close down for any break. The instruction is ongoing.

We must remember that this journey is about progress not perfection. We will occasionally be confronted with those things that have always been there. The usual frustrations, people, and circumstances that challenge us will occasionally surface. However, with a new understanding and desire for peace and personal development, we are better equipped to handle the conflicts and move toward a better place. I am not impervious to pain and attack, just better prepared, and I must always keep training to better my skills.

It is my appreciation in a new light that helps me walk on when things seem insurmountable. My trust in something greater makes me aware I am not alone. I challenge myself daily to remain aware of being the person I should be to those I love if I am to be worthy of their love. I have to accept that life happens and I do not have to like it, but have to either accept it or work on it to the best of my ability. I also want to maintain an appreciation for what is transpiring before my eyes right now, break off my rearview mirror and put tomorrow on hold until it arrives. I also realize I am not alone in this. I have resources and friends. I hope in reading these words, you realize you, too, are not alone. Try to create the life you deserve. With some practice and a few simple skills, you can be an Artisan of the Human Spirit.

About the Title

I will briefly explain how I chose the title *Artisan of the Human Spirit*. By most dictionary definitions, an "artisan" is one who is a craftsman and/or someone who is skilled at applying a certain art or craft. I chose **Artisan** because I believe our state is what determines much of our future, our perception of life, and often requires a degree of restorative work. I think of a craftsman as someone who labors out of skill and love. No two better qualities for what I needed to start some work on myself.

We need to develop our craft and our eye to apply the proper skills of creation, development, and restoration in both creating and maintaining the masterpiece of our lives. We must be able to stand back and nod in approval at our work and not get hung up on every stroke of the brush or pound of the chisel. We are, indeed, our own greatest work of art.

The next part of the title, ***of the***, is not only to commit to elevating your own spirit, but also of those you encounter. Spirituality and joy without connection to others would be like a one-person birthday party. It can be nice, but not quite the same as sharing it with others. Unification of our energies leverages not only our true potential, but also our life's calling. It is not artisan of my, your, his or her human spirit, but ***the*** human spirit in general.

The next component is the human element. By **Human**, I am talking about that which makes us human, our humanity, and our connection to others. Oftentimes we describe being human by our faults. For example, when a mistake or bad judgment is made, we may say, "Hey, I'm only human!" That is true to a degree, but my focus is on the positive aspects of what makes us human: courage, compassion, wisdom, strength, and the elements that bond our species for the better is where I choose to focus my attention. So when I say human, I don't want to limit the scope to only our faults but rather include that which makes us shine.

Spirit has many applications and adaptations from the metaphysical to the religious. My reference is to the *essence* inside each of us that makes us want to connect to our fellow man; that which helps us soar in the face of adversity, that part of us which is Divine.

Since this element can be personally interpreted in many ways, I invite you to define this concept as you feel most comfortable.

So, a lengthier and more descriptive title would be: *My Quest to Create, Restore, and Admire The Masterpiece of My Life And to be In Service to Others, Aiding in My Connection, Love, Compassion and Acceptance of all Humanity, As Well As What Energizes Us and Connects Us to The Divine!* (This wouldn't fit on the cover.)

Regardless of the title, I hope this book gives you insight and inspiration. Thanks for accompanying me on my journey!

It is only when I stopped searching; I started to find everything I had ever searched for!

~ Tony Anders

Quotes used at the beginning of each chapter are what my friends refer to as "Tony-isms."

Further essays and musings by the author can be found at:
http://artisanofthehumanspirit.blogspot.com/
www.tonyanders.com

www.ingramcontent.com/pod-product-compliance
Lightning Source LLC
Chambersburg PA
CBHW022102160426
43198CB00008B/319